gRPC: Up and Running
Building Cloud Native Applications with Go and Java for Docker and Kubernetes

Kasun Indrasiri and Danesh Kuruppu

Beijing · Boston · Farnham · Sebastopol · Tokyo

gRPC: Up and Running

by Kasun Indrasiri and Danesh Kuruppu

Published by O'Reilly Media, Inc., 1005 Gravenstein Highway North, Sebastopol, CA 95472.

O'Reilly books may be purchased for educational, business, or sales promotional use. Online editions are also available for most titles (*http://oreilly.com*). For more information, contact our corporate/institutional sales department: 800-998-9938 or *corporate@oreilly.com*.

Acquisitions Editor: Ryan Shaw	**Indexer:** WordCo Indexing Services, Inc.
Development Editor: Melissa Potter	**Interior Designer:** David Futato
Production Editor: Deborah Baker	**Cover Designer:** Karen Montgomery
Copyeditor: Charles Roumeliotis	**Illustrators:** Rebecca Demarest and Jenny Bergman
Proofreader: Kim Cofer	

February 2020:   First Edition

Revision History for the First Edition

2020-01-23:   First Release

See *http://oreilly.com/catalog/errata.csp?isbn=9781492058335* for release details.

978-1-492-05833-5

[LSI]

Table of Contents

Preface

Nowadays software applications are often connected with each other over computer networks using inter-process communication technologies. gRPC is a modern inter-process communication style based on high-performance RPCs (remote procedure calls) for building distributed applications and microservices. With the advent of microservices and cloud native applications, the adoption of gRPC is exponentially growing.

Why Did We Write This Book?

With the increasing adoption of gRPC, we felt that developers need a comprehensive book on gRPC, a book that you can use as the ultimate reference guide in every stage of the development cycle of your gRPC applications. There are a lot of resources and code samples for gRPC all over the place (documentation, blogs, articles, conference talks, and so on), but there's no single resource that you can use to build gRPC applications. Also, there aren't any resources on the internals of the gRPC protocol and how it works under the hood.

We wrote this book to overcome those challenges and give you a comprehensive understanding of the fundamentals of gRPC, how it differs from conventional inter-process communication technologies, real-world gRPC communication patterns, how to build gRPC applications using Go and Java, how it works under the hood, how to run gRPC applications in production, and how gRPC works with Kubernetes and the rest of the ecosystem.

Who Is This Book For?

The book is most directly relevant to developers who are building distributed applications and microservices using different inter-process communication technologies. When it comes to building such applications and services, developers need to learn the fundamentals of gRPC, when and how to use it for inter-service communication, best practices for running gRPC services in production, and so on. Also, architects who are adopting microservices or cloud native architecture and designing how the services should communicate will get a lot of insight from the book because it compares and contrasts gRPC with other technologies and provides guidelines on when to use and when to avoid it.

We assume that both developers and architects have a basic understanding of the fundamentals of distributed computing such as inter-process communication techniques, service-oriented architecture (SOA), and microservices.

How This Book Is Organized

The book is written in such a way that the theoretical concepts are explained using real-world use cases. Throughout the book, we have extensively used code examples featuring Go and Java to give readers hands-on experience with each of the concepts that they learn. We have organized the book into eight chapters.

Chapter 1

This chapter gives you a basic understanding of gRPC fundamentals and compares it with similar inter-process communication styles such as REST, GraphQL, and other RPC technologies.

Chapter 2

This chapter is where you get the first hands-on experience with building a complete gRPC application using either Go or Java.

Chapter 3

In this chapter, you will explore gRPC communication patterns using real-world examples.

Chapter 4

If you are an advanced gRPC user interested in knowing the internals of gRPC, this is the chapter to learn them. This chapter teaches you every step of gRPC communication between server and client and how it works over the network.

Chapter 5

This chapter teaches you some of the most important advanced features of gRPC such as interceptors, deadlines, metadata, multiplexing, load balancing, and so on.

Chapter 6

This chapter gives you a comprehensive understanding of how to secure communication channels and how we authenticate and control the access of users to gRPC applications.

Chapter 7

This chapter walks you through the entire development life cycle of gRPC applications. We cover testing gRPC applications, integration with CI/CD, deploying and running on Docker and Kubernetes, and observing gRPC applications.

Chapter 8

In this chapter, we discuss some of the helpful supporting components built around gRPC. Most of these projects are useful when building real-world applications using gRPC.

Using Code Examples

All the code examples and supplemental materials for this book are available for download at *https://grpc-up-and-running.github.io*. We highly recommend trying out the samples available in this repository as you are reading the book. It will give you a better understanding of the concepts that you're learning.

These code examples are maintained and kept up to date with the latest versions of the libraries, dependencies, and development tools. Occasionally you may find that the code examples in the text and the examples in the repository slightly differ. We highly encourage you to send a pull request (PR) if you come across any issues or improvements related to the code samples.

You may use this book's example code in your own programs and documentation. You do not need to contact us for permission unless you're reproducing a significant portion of the code. For example, writing a program that uses several chunks of code from this book does not require permission. Selling or distributing examples from O'Reilly books does require permission. Answering a question by citing this book and quoting example code does not require permission. Incorporating a significant amount of example code from this book into your product's documentation does require permission.

We appreciate, but generally do not require, attribution. An attribution usually includes the title, author, publisher, and ISBN. For example: "*gRPC: Up and Running* by Kasun Indrasiri and Danesh Kuruppu (O'Reilly). Copyright 2020 Kasun Indrasiri and Danesh Kuruppu, 978-1-492-05833-5."

If you feel your use of code examples falls outside fair use or the permission given above, feel free to contact us at *permissions@oreilly.com*.

Conventions Used in This Book

The following typographical conventions are used in this book:

Italic
> Indicates new terms, URLs, email addresses, filenames, and file extensions.

`Constant width`
> Used for program listings, as well as within paragraphs to refer to program elements such as variable or function names, databases, data types, environment variables, statements, and keywords.

`Constant width bold`
> Shows commands or other text that should be typed literally by the user.

`Constant width italic`
> Shows text that should be replaced with user-supplied values or by values determined by context.

 This element signifies a tip or suggestion.

 This element signifies a general note.

 This element indicates a warning or caution.

O'Reilly Online Learning

 For more than 40 years, *O'Reilly Media* has provided technology and business training, knowledge, and insight to help companies succeed.

Our unique network of experts and innovators share their knowledge and expertise through books, articles, conferences, and our online learning platform. O'Reilly's online learning platform gives you on-demand access to live training courses, in-depth learning paths, interactive coding environments, and a vast collection of text and video from O'Reilly and 200+ other publishers. For more information, please visit *http://oreilly.com*.

How to Contact Us

Please address comments and questions concerning this book to the publisher:

O'Reilly Media, Inc.
1005 Gravenstein Highway North
Sebastopol, CA 95472
800-998-9938 (in the United States or Canada)
707-829-0515 (international or local)
707-829-0104 (fax)

We have a web page for this book, where we list errata, examples, and any additional information. You can access this page at *https://oreil.ly/gRPC_Up_and_Running*.

Email *bookquestions@oreilly.com* to comment or ask technical questions about this book.

For more information about our books, courses, conferences, and news, see our website at *http://www.oreilly.com*.

Find us on Facebook: *http://facebook.com/oreilly*

Follow us on Twitter: *http://twitter.com/oreillymedia*

Watch us on YouTube: *http://www.youtube.com/oreillymedia*

Acknowledgments

Our grateful thanks go to the tech reviewers of this book, Julien Andrieux, Tim Raymond, and Ryan Michela. Also, we would like to thank our Development Editor Melissa Potter for her guidance and support, and our Acquisitions Editor Ryan Shaw for all the support given. Last but not least we thank the entire gRPC community for creating such a great open source project.

CHAPTER 1

Introduction to gRPC

Modern software applications rarely operate in isolation. Rather, they are connected with each other through computer networks and communicate and coordinate their actions by passing messages to one another. Therefore, a modern software system is a collection of distributed software applications that are running at different network locations and communicate with each other with message passing using different communication protocols. For example, an online retail software system comprises multiple distributed applications such as an order management application, catalog application, databases, and so on. To implement the business functionalities of an online retail system, it is required to have interconnectivity between those distributed applications.

Microservices Architecture

Microservices architecture is about building a software application as a collection of independent, autonomous (developed, deployed, and scaled independently), business capability–oriented, and loosely coupled services.[1]

With the advent of microservices architecture (*https://oreil.ly/q6N1P*) and cloud native architecture (*https://oreil.ly/8Ow2T*), conventional software applications that are built for multiple business capabilities are further segregated into a collection of fine-grained, autonomous, and business capability–oriented entities known as micro-services. Therefore, a microservices-based software system also requires the micro-services to be connected through the network using inter-process (or inter-service or inter-application) communication techniques. As an example, if we consider the same

---

1 K. Indrasiri and P. Siriwardena, *Microservices for the Enterprise* (Apress, 2018).

online retail system implemented using microservices architecture, you will find multiple interconnected microservices such as order management, search, checkout, shipping, and so on. Unlike conventional applications, the number of network communication links proliferates because of the fine-grained nature of microservices. Therefore, no matter the architectural style (conventional or microservices architecture) you use, inter-process communication techniques are one of the most important aspects of modern distributed software applications.

Inter-process communications are usually implemented using message passing with a synchronous request-response style or asynchronous event-driven styles. In the synchronous communication style, the client process sends a request message to the server process over the network and waits for a response message. In asynchronous event-driven messaging, processes communicate with asynchronous message passing by using an intermediary known as an *event broker*. Depending on your business use case, you can select the communication pattern that you want to implement.

When it comes to building synchronous request-response style communication for modern cloud native applications and microservices, the most common and conventional approach is to build them as RESTful services, where you model your application or service as a collection of resources that can be accessed and have their state changed via network calls that take place over the HTTP protocol. However, for most use cases RESTful services are quite bulky, inefficient, and error-prone for building inter-process communication. It is often required to have a highly scalable, loosely coupled inter-process communication technology that is more efficient than RESTful services. This is where gRPC, a modern inter-process communication style for building distributed applications and microservices, comes into the picture (we'll compare and contrast gRPC with RESTful communication later in this chapter). gRPC primarily uses a synchronous request-response style for communication but can operate in fully asynchronous or streaming mode once the initial communication is established.

In this chapter, we'll explore what gRPC is and the key motivations behind inventing such an inter-process communication protocol. We dive into the key building blocks of the gRPC protocol with the help of some real-world use cases. Also, it's important to have a solid understanding of inter-process communication techniques and how they have evolved over time so that you can understand the key problems that gRPC is trying to solve. So, we'll walk through those techniques and compare and contrast each of them. Let's begin our discussion on gRPC by looking at what gRPC is.

What Is gRPC?

gRPC (the "g" stands for something different in every gRPC release (*https://oreil.ly/IKCi3*)) is an inter-process communication technology that allows you to connect, invoke, operate, and debug distributed heterogeneous applications as easily as making a local function call.

When you develop a gRPC application the first thing that you do is define a service interface. The service interface definition contains information on how your service can be consumed by consumers, what methods you allow the consumers to call remotely, what method parameters and message formats to use when invoking those methods, and so on. The language that we specify in the service definition is known as an *interface definition language* (IDL).

Using that service definition, you can generate the server-side code known as a *server skeleton*, which simplifies the server-side logic by providing low-level communication abstractions. Also, you can generate the client-side code, known as a *client stub*, which simplifies the client-side communication with abstractions to hide low-level communication for different programming languages. The methods that you specify in the service interface definition can be remotely invoked by the client side as easily as making a local function invocation. The underlying gRPC framework handles all the complexities that are normally associated with enforcing strict service contracts, data serialization, network communication, authentication, access control, observability, and so on.

To understand the fundamental concepts of gRPC, let's take a look at a real-world use case of a microservice implemented with gRPC. Suppose we are building an online retail application comprised of multiple microservices. As illustrated in Figure 1-1, suppose that we want to build a microservice that gives the details of the products that are available in our online retail application (we will implement this use case from the ground up in Chapter 2). The ProductInfo service is modeled in such a way that it is exposed over the network as a gRPC service.

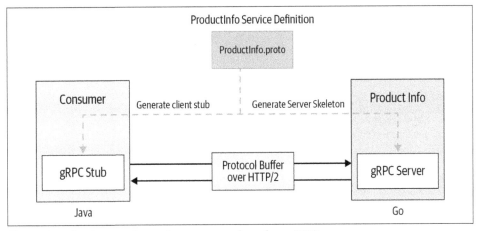

Figure 1-1. A microservice and a consumer based on gRPC

The service definition is specified in the *ProductInfo.proto* file, which is used by both the server and client sides to generate the code. In this example, we have assumed that the service is implemented using the Go language and that the consumer is implemented using Java. The network communication between the service and con-sumer takes place over HTTP/2.

Now let's delve into the details of this gRPC communication. The first step of building a gRPC service is to create the service interface definition with the methods that are exposed by that service along with input parameters and return types. Let's move on to the details of the service definition.

Service Definition

gRPC uses protocol buffers (*https://oreil.ly/iFi-b*) as the IDL to define the service interface. Protocol buffers are a language-agnostic, platform-neutral, extensible mechanism to serializing structured data (we'll cover some of the fundamentals of protocol buffers in detail in Chapter 4, but for now you can think of it as a data serial-ization mechanism). The service interface definition is specified in a proto file—an ordinary text file with a *.proto* extension. You define gRPC services in ordinary proto-col buffer format, with RPC method parameters and return types specified as proto-col buffer messages. Since the service definition is an extension to the protocol buffer specification, a special gRPC plug-in is used to generate code from your proto file.

In our example use case, the ProductInfo service's interface can be defined using pro-tocol buffers as shown in Example 1-1. The service definition of ProductInfo is com-prised of a service interface definition where we specify the remote methods, their input and output parameters, and the type definition (or message formats) of those parameters.

Example 1-1. gRPC service definition of ProductInfo service using protocol buffers

```
// ProductInfo.proto
syntax = "proto3"; ❶
package ecommerce; ❷

service ProductInfo { ❸
    rpc addProduct(Product) returns (ProductID); ❹
    rpc getProduct(ProductID) returns (Product); ❺
}

message Product { ❻
    string id = 1; ❼
    string name = 2;
    string description = 3;
}

message ProductID { ❽
    string value = 1;
}
```

❶ The service definition begins with specifying the protocol buffer version (proto3) that we use.

❷ Package names are used to prevent name clashes between protocol message types and also will be used to generate code.

❸ Defining the service interface of a gRPC service.

❹ Remote method to add a product that returns the product ID as the response.

❺ Remote method to get a product based on the product ID.

❻ Definition of the message format/type of `Product`.

❼ Field (name-value pair) that holds the product ID with unique field numbers that are used to identify your fields in the message binary format.

❽ User-defined type for product identification number.

A service is thus a collection of methods (e.g., `addProduct` and `getProduct`) that can be remotely invoked. Each method has input parameters and return types that we define as either part of the service or that can be imported into the protocol buffer definition.

The input and return parameters can be a user-defined type (e.g., `Product` and `Pro ductID` types) or a protocol buffer well-known type (*https://oreil.ly/0Uc3A*) defined in the service definition. Those types are structured as messages, where each message is a small logical record of information containing a series of name-value pairs called fields. These fields are name-value pairs with unique field numbers (e.g., `string id = 1`) that are used to identify your fields in the message binary format.

This service definition is used to build the server and client side of your gRPC application. In the next section, we'll go into the details of gRPC server implementation.

gRPC Server

Once you have a service definition in place, you can use it to generate the server- or client-side code using the protocol buffer compiler *protoc*. With the gRPC plug-in for protocol buffers, you can generate gRPC server-side and client-side code, as well as the regular protocol buffer code for populating, serializing, and retrieving your message types.

On the server side, the server implements that service definition and runs a gRPC server to handle client calls. Therefore, on the server side, to make the `ProductInfo` service do its job you need to do the following:

1. Implement the service logic of the generated service skeleton by overriding the service base class.

2. Run a gRPC server to listen for requests from clients and return the service responses.

When implementing service logic, the first thing to do is generate the service skeleton from the service definition. For example, in the code snippet in Example 1-2, you can find the generated remote functions for the ProductInfo service built with Go. Inside the body of these remote functions you can implement the logic of each function.

Example 1-2. gRPC server-side implementation of ProductInfo service with Go

```
import (
  ...
  "context"
  pb "github.com/grpc-up-and-running/samples/ch02/productinfo/go/proto"
  "google.golang.org/grpc"
  ...
)

// ProductInfo implementation with Go

// Add product remote method
func (s *server) AddProduct(ctx context.Context, in *pb.Product) (
      *pb.ProductID, error) {
  // business logic
}

// Get product remote method
func (s *server) GetProduct(ctx context.Context, in *pb.ProductID) (
     *pb.Product, error) {
  // business logic
}
```

Once you have the service implementation ready, you need to run a gRPC server to listen for requests from clients, dispatch those requests to the service implementation, and return the service responses back to the client. The code snippet in Example 1-3 shows a gRPC server implementation with Go for the ProductInfo service use case. Here we open up a TCP port, start the gRPC server, and register the ProductInfo service with that server.

Example 1-3. Running a gRPC server for ProductInfo service with Go

```
func main() {
  lis, _ := net.Listen("tcp", port)
  s := grpc.NewServer()
  pb.RegisterProductInfoServer(s, &server{})
```

```
  if err := s.Serve(lis); err != nil {
    log.Fatalf("failed to serve: %v", err)
  }
}
```

That's all you have to do on the server side. Let's move on to the gRPC client-side implementation.

gRPC Client

Similar to the server side, we can generate the client-side stub using the service definition. The client stub provides the same methods as the server, which your client code can invoke; the client stub translates them to remote function invocation network calls that go to the server side. Since gRPC service definitions are language-agnostic, you can generate clients and servers for any supported language (via the third-party implementations (*https://oreil.ly/psi72*)) of your choice. So for the Produc tInfo service use case, we can generate the client stub for Java while our server side is implemented with Go. In the code snippet in Example 1-4, you find the code for Java. Despite the programming language we use, the simple steps involved in a client-side implementation involve setting up a connection with the remote server, attaching the client stub with that connection, and invoking the remote method using the client stub.

Example 1-4. gRPC client to invoke a remote method of service

```
// Create a channel using remote server address
ManagedChannel channel = ManagedChannelBuilder.forAddress("localhost", 8080)
    .usePlaintext(true)
    .build();

// Initialize blocking stub using the channel
ProductInfoGrpc.ProductInfoBlockingStub stub =
        ProductInfoGrpc.newBlockingStub(channel);

// Call remote method using the blocking stub
StringValue productID = stub.addProduct(
        Product.newBuilder()
        .setName("Apple iPhone 11")
        .setDescription("Meet Apple iPhone 11." +
            "All-new dual-camera system with " +
            "Ultra Wide and Night mode.")
        .build());
```

As you now have a good sense of the key concepts of gRPC, let's try to understand the gRPC client–server message flow in detail.

Client–Server Message Flow

When a gRPC client invokes a gRPC service, the client-side gRPC library uses the protocol buffer and marshals the remote procedure call protocol buffer format, which is then sent over HTTP/2. On the server side, the request is unmarshaled and the respective procedure invocation is executed using protocol buffers. The response follows a similar execution flow from the server to the client. As the wire transport protocol, gRPC uses HTTP/2, which is a high-performance binary message protocol with support for bidirectional messaging. We will further discuss the low-level details of the message flow between gRPC clients and servers along with protocol buffers and how gRPC uses HTTP/2 in Chapter 4.

 Marshaling is the process of packing parameters and a remote function into a message packet that is sent over the network, while unmarshaling unpacks the message packet into the respective method invocation.

Before we go further into the gRPC protocol, it's important to have a broad understanding of different inter-process communication technologies and how they have evolved with time.

Evolution of Inter-Process Communication

Inter-process communication techniques have been drastically evolving over time. There are various such techniques emerging to address modern needs and to provide a better and more efficient development experience. So, it's important to have a good understanding of how inter-process communication techniques have evolved and how they made their way to gRPC. Let's look at some of the most commonly used inter-process communication techniques and try to compare and contrast them with gRPC.

Conventional RPC

RPC was a popular inter-process communication technique for building client-service applications. With RPC a client can remotely invoke a function of a method just like calling a local method. There were popular RPC implementations in the early days such as the Common Object Request Broker Architecture (CORBA) and Java Remote Method Invocation (RMI), which were used for building and connecting services or applications. However, most such conventional RPC implementations are overwhelmingly complex, as they are built on top of communication protocols such as TCP, which hinders interoperability, and are based on bloated specifications.

SOAP

Owing to the limitations of conventional RPC implementations such as CORBA, Simple Object Access Protocol (SOAP) was designed and heavily promoted by large-scale enterprises such as Microsoft, IBM, etc. SOAP is the standard communication technique in a service-oriented architecture (SOA) to exchange XML-based structured data between services (usually called web services in the context of SOA) and communicates over any underlying communication protocol such as HTTP (most commonly used).

With SOAP you can define the service interface, operations of that service, and an associated XML message format to be used to invoke those operations. SOAP was quite a popular technology but the complexity of message format, as well as the complexities of specifications built around SOAP, hinders the agility of building distributed applications. Therefore, in the context of modern distributed application development, SOAP web services are considered a legacy technology. Rather than using SOAP, most of the existing distributed applications are now being developed using the REST architecture style.

REST

Representational State Transfer (REST) is an architectural style that originated from Roy Fielding's PhD dissertation (*https://oreil.ly/6tRrt*). Fielding is one of the principal authors of the HTTP specification and the originator of the REST architectural style. REST is the foundation of the resource-oriented architecture (ROA), where you model distributed applications as a collection of resources and the clients that access those resources can change the state (create, read, update, or delete) of those resources.

The de facto implementation of REST is HTTP, and in HTTP you can model a RESTful web application as a collection of resources accessible using a unique identifier (URL). The state-changing operations are applied on top of those resources in the form of the HTTP verbs (GET, POST, PUT, DELETE, PATCH, and so on). The resource state is represented in textual formats such as JSON, XML, HTML, YAML, and so on.

Building applications using the REST architectural style with HTTP and JSON has become the de facto method of building microservices. However, with the proliferation of the number of microservices and their network interactions RESTful services have not been able to meet the expected modern requirements. There are a couple of key limitations of RESTful services that hinder the ability to use them as the messaging protocol for modern microservices-based applications.

Inefficient text-based message protocols

Inherently, RESTful services are built on top of text-based transport protocols such as HTTP 1.x and leverage human-readable textual formats such as JSON. When it comes to service-to-service communication, it is quite inefficient to use a textual format such as JSON because both parties to that communication do not need to use such human-readable textual formats.

The client application (source) produces binary content to be sent to the server, then it converts the binary structure into text (because with HTTP 1.x you have to send textual messages) and sends it over the network in text (over HTTP) to a machine that parses and turns it back into a binary structure on the service (target) side. Rather, we could have easily sent a binary format that can be mapped to a service's and consumer's business logic. One popular argument for using JSON is that it is easier to use because it's "human-readable." This is more a tooling problem than a problem with the binary protocols.

Lacks strongly typed interfaces between apps

With the increasing number of services interacting over the network that are built with disparate polyglot technologies, the lack of well-defined and strongly typed service definitions was a major setback. Most of the existing service definition technologies that we have in RESTful services, such as OpenAPI/Swagger, are afterthoughts and not tightly integrated with the underlying architectural style or messaging protocols.

This leads to many incompatibilities, runtime errors, and interoperability issues in building such decentralized applications. For instance, when you develop RESTful services, it is not required to have a service definition and type definition of the information that is shared between the applications. Rather, you develop your RESTful applications either looking at the textual format on the wire or third-party API definition technologies such as OpenAPI. Therefore, having a modern strongly typed service definition technology and a framework that generates the core of the server- and client-side code for polyglot technologies is a key necessity.

REST architectural style is hard to enforce

As an architectural style, REST has a lot of "good practices" that you need to follow to make a real RESTful service. But they are not enforced as part of the implementation protocols (such as HTTP), which makes it hard to enforce them at the implementation phase. Therefore, in practice, most of the services that claim to be RESTful are not properly following the foundations of the REST style. So, most of the so-called RESTful services are merely HTTP services exposed over the network. Therefore, development teams have to spend a lot of time maintaining the consistency and purity of a RESTful service.

With all these limitations of inter-process communication techniques in building modern cloud native applications, the quest for inventing a better message protocol began.

Inception of gRPC

Google had been using a general-purpose RPC framework called *Stubby* (*https:// oreil.ly/vat5r*) to connect thousands of microservices that are running across multiple data centers and built with disparate technologies. Its core RPC layer was designed to handle an internet scale of tens of billions of requests per second. Stubby has many great features, but it is not standardized to be used as a generic framework as it is too tightly coupled to Google's internal infrastructure.

In 2015, Google released (*https://oreil.ly/cUZSG*) gRPC as an open source RPC framework; it is a standardized, general-purpose, and cross-platform RPC infrastructure. gRPC was intended to provide the same scalability, performance, and functionality that Stubby offered, but to the community at large.

Since then, the popularity of gRPC has grown dramatically over the past few years with large-scale adoption from major companies such as Netflix, Square, Lyft, Docker, Cisco, and CoreOS. Later, gRPC joined (*https://oreil.ly/GFffo*) the Cloud Native Computing Foundation (CNCF), one of the most popular open source software foundations dedicated to making cloud native computing universal and sustainable; gRPC gained a lot of traction from CNCF ecosystem projects.

Now let's look at some of the key reasons for using gRPC over the conventional inter-process communication protocols.

Why gRPC?

gRPC is designed to be an internet-scale, inter-process communication technology that can overcome most of the shortcomings of conventional inter-process communication technologies. Owing to the benefits of gRPC, most modern applications and servers are increasingly converting their inter-process communication protocol to gRPC. So, why would somebody select gRPC as a communication protocol when there are so many other options available? Let's look more closely at some of the key advantages that gRPC brings to the table.

Advantages of gRPC

The advantages that gRPC brings are key to the increasing adoption of gRPC. These advantages include the following:

It's efficient for inter-process communication
Rather than using a textual format such as JSON or XML, gRPC uses a protocol buffer–based binary protocol to communicate with gRPC services and clients.

Also, gRPC implements protocol buffers on top of HTTP/2, which makes it even faster for inter-process communication. This makes gRPC one of the most efficient inter-process communication technologies out there.

It has simple, well-defined service interfaces and schema
gRPC fosters a contract-first approach for developing applications. You first define the service interfaces and then work on the implementation details afterward. So, unlike OpenAPI/Swagger for RESTful service definition and WSDL for SOAP web services, gRPC offers a simple but consistent, reliable, and scalable application development experience.

It's strongly typed
Since we use protocol buffers to define gRPC services, gRPC service contracts clearly define the types that you will be using for communication between the applications. This makes distributed application development much more stable, as static typing helps to overcome most of the runtime and interoperability errors that you would encounter when you build cloud native applications that span across multiple teams and technologies.

It's polyglot
gRPC is designed to work with multiple programming languages. A gRPC service definition with protocol buffers is language-agnostic. Hence, you can pick the language of your choice but can interoperate with any existing gRPC service or client.

It has duplex streaming
gRPC has native support for client- or server-side streaming, which is baked into the service definition itself. This makes it much easier to develop streaming services or streaming clients. And the ability to build conventional request–response style messaging and client- and server-side streaming is a key advantage over the conventional RESTful messaging style.

It has built-in commodity features
gRPC offers built-in support for commodity features such as authentication, encryption, resiliency (deadlines and timeouts), metadata exchange, compression, load balancing, service discovery, and so on (we'll explore these in Chapter 5).

It's integrated with cloud native ecosystems
gRPC is part of the CNCF and most of the modern frameworks and technologies offer native support for gRPC out of the box. For instance, many projects under CNCF such as Envoy (*https://oreil.ly/vGQsj*) support gRPC as a communication protocol; for cross-cutting features such as metrics and monitoring, gRPC is supported by most such tools (e.g., using Prometheus (*https://oreil.ly/AU3-7*) to monitor gRPC applications).

It's mature and has been widely adopted
> gRPC has been matured by its heavy battle-testing at Google, and many other major tech companies such as Square, Lyft, Netflix, Docker, Cisco, and CoreOS have adopted it.

As with any technology, gRPC comes with a certain set of drawbacks as well. Knowing those drawbacks during application development is quite useful. So, let's take a look at some of the limitations of gRPC.

Disadvantages of gRPC

Here are some of the disadvantages of gRPC that you need to be mindful of when you select it for building applications. These include the following:

It may not be suitable for external-facing services
> When you want to expose the application or services to an external client over the internet, gRPC may not be the most suitable protocol as most of the external consumers are quite newly about gRPC and REST/HTTP. The contract-driven, strongly typed nature of gRPC services may hinder the flexibility of the services that you expose to the external parties, and consumers get far less control (unlike protocols such as GraphQL, which is explained in the next section). The gRPC gateway is designed as a workaround to overcome this issue. We'll discuss it in detail in Chapter 8.

Drastic service definition changes are a complicated development process
> Schema modifications are quite common in modern inter-service communication use cases. When there are drastic gRPC service definition changes, usually we need to regenerate code for both client and server. This needs to be incorporated into the existing continuous integration process and may complicate the overall development life cycle. However, most gRPC service definition changes can be accommodated without breaking the service contract, and gRPC will happily interoperate with clients and servers using different versions of a proto, as long as no breaking changes are introduced. So code regeneration is not required in most cases.

The ecosystem is relatively small
> The gRPC ecosystem is still relatively small compared to the conventional REST/HTTP protocol. The support for gRPC in browser and mobile applications is still in the primitive stages.

You must be mindful about these limitations when it comes to the development of applications. So, obviously, gRPC is not a technique that you should use for all your inter-process communication requirements. Rather, you need to evaluate the business use case and requirements and pick the appropriate messaging protocol. We'll explore some of these guidelines in Chapter 8.

As we discussed in previous sections, there are many existing and emerging inter-process communication techniques out there. It's important to have a good understanding of how we can compare gRPC with other similar technologies that have gained popularity in the modern application development landscape, as this will help you in finding the most appropriate protocol for your services.

gRPC Versus Other Protocols: GraphQL and Thrift

We have discussed in detail some of the key limitations of REST, which laid the foundation to the inception of gRPC. Similarly, there are quite a few inter-process communication technologies emerging to fulfill the same needs. So, let's look at some of the popular technologies and compare them with gRPC.

Apache Thrift

Apache Thrift (*https://thrift.apache.org*) is an RPC framework (initially developed at Facebook and later donated to Apache) similar to gRPC. It uses its own interface definition language and offers support for a wide range of programming languages. Thrift allows you to define data types and service interfaces in a definition file. By taking the service definition as the input, the Thrift compiler generates code for the client and server sides. The Thrift transport layer provides abstractions for network I/O and decouples Thrift from the rest of the system, which means it can run on any transport implementation such as TCP, HTTP, and so on.

If you compare Thrift with gRPC, you will find both pretty much follow the same design and usage goals. However, there are several important differentiators between the two:

Transport
> gRPC is more opinionated than Thrift and offers first-class support for HTTP/2. Its implementations on HTTP/2 leverage the protocol's capabilities to achieve efficiency and support for messaging patterns such as streaming.

Streaming
> gRPC service definitions natively support bidirectional streaming (client and server) as part of the service definition itself.

Adoption and community
> When it comes to adoption gRPC seems to have a pretty good momentum and has managed to build a good ecosystem around CNCF projects. Also, community resources such as good documentation, external presentations, and sample use cases are quite common for gRPC, which makes the adoption process smooth compared to Thrift.

Performance

While there are no official results comparing gRPC versus Thrift, there are a few online resources with performance comparisons between the two that show better numbers for Thrift. However, gRPC is also being heavily benchmarked for performance in almost all releases (*https://oreil.ly/Hy3mJ*). So performance is unlikely to be a deciding factor when it comes to selecting Thrift over gRPC. Also, there are other RPC frameworks that offer similar capabilities but gRPC is currently leading the way as the most standardized, interoperable, and widely adopted RPC technology.

GraphQL

GraphQL (*https://graphql.org*) is another technology (invented by Facebook and standardized as an open technology) that is becoming quite popular for building inter-process communication. It is a query language for APIs and a runtime for fulfilling those queries with your existing data. GraphQL offers a fundamentally different approach for conventional client–server communication by allowing clients to determine what data they want, how they want it, and in what format they want it. gRPC, on the other hand, has a fixed contract for the remote methods that enable communication between the client and the server.

GraphQL is more suitable for external-facing services or APIs that are exposed to consumers directly where the clients need more control over the data that consume from the server. For example, in our online retail application scenario, suppose that the consumers of the ProductInfo service need only specific information about the products but not the entire set of attributes of a product, and the consumers also need a way to specify the information they want. With GraphQL you can model a service so that it allows consumers to query the service using the GraphQL query language and obtain the required information.

In most of the pragmatic use cases of GraphQL and gRPC, GraphQL is being used for external-facing services/APIs while internal services that are backing the APIs are implemented using gRPC.

Now let's have a look at some of the real-world adopters of gRPC and their use cases.

gRPC in the Real World

The success of any inter-process communication protocol is largely dependent on industry-wide adoption and the user and developer community behind that project. gRPC has been widely adopted for building microservices and cloud native applications. Let's look at some of the key success stories of gRPC.

Netflix

Netflix (*https://oreil.ly/xK3Ds*), a subscription-based video streaming company, is one of the pioneers in practicing microservices architecture at scale. All of its video streaming capabilities are offered to consumers through an external-facing managed service (or APIs) and there are hundreds of backend services that are backing its APIs. Therefore, inter-process (or inter-service) communication is one of the most important aspects of its use case. During the initial stage of microservices implementation, Netflix developed its own technology stack for inter-service communication using RESTful services on HTTP/1.1, which backs almost 98% of the business use cases of the Netflix product.

However, Netflix has observed several limitations of the RESTful services–based approach when they operate at internet scale. The consumers of RESTful microservices were often written from scratch by inspecting the resources and required message formats of the RESTful services. This was very time-consuming, hindered developer productivity, and also increased the risk for more error-prone code. Service implementation and consumption was also challenging because of the lack of technologies for a comprehensive definition of a service interface. So, it initially tried to overcome most of these limitations by building an internal RPC framework, but after evaluating available technology stacks, it chose gRPC as its inter-service communication technology. During its evaluation, Netflix found that gRPC was comfortably at the top in terms of encapsulating all the required responsibilities together in one easy-to-consume package.

With the adoption of gRPC, Netflix has seen a massive boost in developer productivity. For example, for each client, hundreds of lines of custom code are replaced by just two to three lines of configuration in the proto. Creating a client, which could take up to two to three weeks, takes a matter of minutes with gRPC. The overall stability of the platform has also improved a lot because handwritten code for most of the commodity features is no longer needed and there is a comprehensive and safe way of defining service interfaces. Owing to the performance boost that gRPC provides, the overall latency of Netflix's entire platform has reduced. Since it has adopted gRPC for most of its inter-process communication use cases, it seems that Netflix has put some of its homegrown projects (for example, Ribbon (*https://oreil.ly/qKgv4*)) that are built for inter-process communication using REST and HTTP protocols into maintenance mode (not in active development) and are using gRPC instead.

etcd

etcd (*https://oreil.ly/wo4gM*) is a distributed reliable key-value store for the most critical data of a distributed system. It's one of the most popular open source projects in CNCF and heavily adopted by many other open source projects such as Kubernetes. One key factor in gRPC's success is that it has a simple, well-defined, easy-to-consume, user-facing API. etcd uses a gRPC user-facing API (*https://oreil.ly/v-H-K*) to leverage the full power of gRPC.

Dropbox

Dropbox is a file-hosting service that offers cloud storage, file synchronization, personal cloud, and client software. Dropbox runs hundreds of polyglot microservices, which exchange millions of requests per second. It was using multiple RPC frameworks initially, including a homegrown RPC framework with a custom protocol for manual serialization and deserialization, Apache Thrift, and a legacy RPC framework that was an HTTP/1.1-based protocol with protobuf-encoded messages.

Rather than using any of those, Dropbox has switched to gRPC (which also allows it to reuse some of the existing protocol buffer definitions of its message formats). It has created Courier (*https://oreil.ly/msjcZ*), a gRPC-based RPC framework. Courier is not a new RPC protocol but a project that integrates gRPC with Dropbox's existing infrastructure. Dropbox has augmented gRPC to cater to its specific requirements related to authentication, authorization, service discovery, service statistics, event logging, and tracing tools.

These success stories of gRPC tell us that it's an inter-process messaging protocol that is simple, boosts productivity and reliability, and scales and operates at the internet scale. These are some of the well-known early adopters of gRPC, but the use cases and adoption of gRPC are increasingly growing.

Summary

Modern software applications or services rarely live in isolation and the inter-process communication techniques that connect them are one of the most important aspects of modern distributed software applications. gRPC is a scalable, loosely coupled, and type-safe solution that allows for more efficient inter-process communication than conventional REST/HTTP-based communication. It allows you to connect, invoke, operate, and debug distributed heterogeneous applications as easy as making a local method call via network transport protocols such as HTTP/2.

gRPC can also be considered as an evolution of conventional RPCs and has managed to overcome their limitations. gRPC is being widely adopted by various internet-scale companies for their inter-process communication requirements and is most commonly used for building internal service-to-service communications.

The knowledge you gain from this chapter will be a good entry point for the rest of the chapters, where you will dive deep into different aspects of gRPC communication. This knowledge will be put into practice in the next chapter where we build a real-world gRPC application from the ground up.

CHAPTER 2

Getting Started with gRPC

Enough with the theory on gRPC; let's apply what you learned in Chapter 1 to build a real-world gRPC application from the ground up. In this chapter, you will use both Go and Java to build a simple gRPC service and a client application that invokes the service you developed. In the process you'll learn about specifying a gRPC service definition using protocol buffers, generating a server skeleton and client stub, implementing a service's business logic, running a gRPC server with the service you implemented, and invoking the service through the gRPC client application.

Let's use the same online retail system from Chapter 1, where we need to build a service that is responsible for managing the products of a retail store. The service can be remotely accessed and the consumers of that service can add new products to the system and also retrieve product details from the system by providing the product ID. We'll model this service and consumer using gRPC. You may pick the programming language of your choice to implement this, but in this chapter, we will use both the Go and Java languages to implement this sample.

 You can try out both the Go and Java implementations of the sample in the source code repository for this book.

In Figure 2-1, we illustrate the client–server communication patterns of the `Produc tInfo` service for each method invocation. The server hosts a gRPC service that offers two remote methods: `addProduct(product)` and `getProduct(productId)`. The client can invoke either of those remote methods.

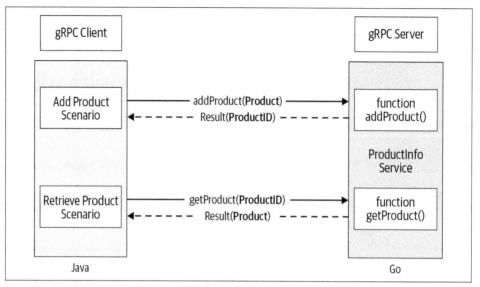

Figure 2-1. Client–server interaction of ProductInfo service

Let's start building this sample by creating the service definition of the ProductInfo gRPC service.

Creating the Service Definition

As you learned in Chapter 1, when you develop a gRPC application, the first thing you do is define the service interface, which contains the methods that allow consumers to call remotely, the method parameters and message formats to use when invoking those methods, and so on. All these service definitions are recorded as a protocol buffer's definition (*https://oreil.ly/1X5Ws*), which is the interface definition language (IDL) used in gRPC.

> We will further dive into service definition techniques for different messaging patterns in Chapter 3. We will also cover the details of protocol buffers and gRPC implementation details in Chapter 4.

Once you identify the business capabilities of the service, you can define the service interface to fulfill the business need. In our sample, we can identify two remote methods (addProduct(product) and getProduct(productId)) in the ProductInfo service and two message types (Product and ProductID) that both methods accept and return.

The next step is to specify these service definitions as a protocol buffer definition. With protocol buffers, we can define services and message types. A service consists of its methods and each method is defined by its type, input, and output parameters. The message consists of its fields and each field is defined by its type and a unique index value. Let's dive into the details of defining message structures.

Defining Messages

The *message* is the data structure that is exchanged between client and service. As you can see in Figure 2-1, our `ProductInfo` use case has two message types. One is the product information (`Product`), which is required when adding a new product to the system and is returned when retrieving a particular product. The other is a unique identification (`ProductID`) of the product, which is required when retrieving a particular product from the system and is returned when adding a new product:

ProductID
> `ProductID` is a unique identifier of the product that can be a string value. We can either define our own message type that contains a string field or use the well-known message type `google.protobuf.StringValue`, provided by the protocol buffer library. In this example, we are going to define our own message type that contains a string field. The `ProductID` message type definition is shown in Example 2-1.

Example 2-1. Protocol Buffer definition of ProductID message type.

```
message ProductID {
    string value = 1;
}
```

Product
> `Product` is a custom message type that represents the data that should exist in a product in our online retail application. It can have a set of fields that represent the data associated with each product. Suppose the `Product` message type has the following fields:

> ID
> > Unique identifier of the product

> Name
> > Product name

> Description
> > Product description

Price
> Product price

Then we can define our custom message type using a protocol buffer as shown in Example 2-2.

Example 2-2. Protocol buffer definition of Product message type

```
message Product {
    string id = 1;
    string name = 2;
    string description = 3;
    float price = 4;
}
```

Here the number assigned to each message field is used to uniquely identify the field in the message. So, we can't use the same number in two different fields in the same message definition. We will further dive into the details of the message definition techniques of protocol buffers and explain why we need to provide a unique number for each field in Chapter 4. For now, you can think of it as a rule when defining a protocol buffer message.

 The protobuf library provides a set of protobuf message types for well-known types. So we can reuse them instead of defining such types again in our service definition. You can get more details about these well-known types in the protocol buffers documentation (*https://oreil.ly/D8Ysn*).

Since we have completed defining message types for the ProductInfo service, we can move on to the service interface definition.

Defining Services

A *service* is a collection of remote methods that are exposed to a client. In our sample, the ProductInfo service has two remote methods: addProduct(product) and get Product(productId). According to the protocol buffer rule, we can only have one input parameter in a remote method and it can return only one value. If we need to pass multiple values to the method like in the addProduct method, we need to define a message type and group all the values as we have done in the Product message type:

addProduct
> Creates a new Product in the system. It requires the details of the product as input and returns the product identification number of the newly added product, if the action completed successfully. Example 2-3 shows the definition of the add Product method.

Example 2-3. Protocol buffer definition of addProduct method

```
rpc addProduct(Product) returns (google.protobuf.StringValue);
```

getProduct
> Retrieves product information. It requires the `ProductID` as input and returns `Product` details if a particular product exists in the system. Example 2-4 shows the definition of the `getProduct` method.

Example 2-4. Protocol buffer definition of getProduct method

```
rpc getProduct(google.protobuf.StringValue) returns (Product);
```

Combining all messages and services, we now have a complete protocol buffer definition for our `ProductInfo` use case, as shown in Example 2-5.

Example 2-5. gRPC service definition of ProductInfo service using protocol buffers

```
syntax = "proto3"; ❶
package ecommerce; ❷

service ProductInfo { ❸
    rpc addProduct(Product) returns (ProductID); ❹
    rpc getProduct(ProductID) returns (Product); ❺
}

message Product { ❻
    string id = 1; ❼
    string name = 2;
    string description = 3;
}

message ProductID { ❽
    string value = 1;
}
```

❶   The service definition begins with specifying the protocol buffer version (proto3) that we use.

❷   Package names are used to prevent name clashes between protocol message types and also will be used to generate code.

❸   Definition of the service interface of the service.

❹   Remote method to add a product that returns the product ID as the response.

❺   Remote method to get a product based on the product ID.

❻ Definition of the message format/type of `Product`.

❼ Field (name-value pair) that holds the product ID with unique field numbers that are used to identify your fields in the message binary format.

❽ Definition of the message format/type of ProductID.

In the protocol buffer definition, we can specify a package name (e.g., `ecommerce`), which helps to prevent naming conflicts between different projects. When we generate code for our services or clients using this service definition with a package, the same packages (unless we explicitly specify a different package for code generation) are created in the respective programming language (of course only if the language supports the notion of a *package*) with which our code is generated. We can also define package names with version numbers like `ecommerce.v1` and `ecommerce.v2`. So future major changes to the API can coexist in the same codebase.

 Commonly used IDEs (integrated development environments) such as IntelliJ IDEA, Eclipse, VSCode, etc., now have plug-ins to support protocol buffers. You can install the plug-in to your IDE and easily create a protocol buffer definition for your service.

One other process that should be mentioned here is importing from another proto file. If we need to use the message types defined in other proto files, we can import them and our protocol buffer definition. For example, if we want to use the `String Value` type (`google.protobuf.StringValue`) defined in the *wrappers.proto* file, we can import the *google/protobuf/wrappers.proto* file in our definition as follows:

```
syntax = "proto3";

import "google/protobuf/wrappers.proto";

package ecommerce;
...
```

Once you complete the specification of the service definition, you can proceed to the implementation of the gRPC service and the client.

Implementation

Let's implement a gRPC service with the set of remote methods that we specified in the service definition. These remote methods are exposed by the server and the gRPC client connects to the server and invokes those remote methods.

As illustrated in Figure 2-2, we first need to compile the `ProductInfo` service definition and generate source code for the chosen language. Out of the box, gRPC is supported by all the popular languages like Java, Go, Python, Ruby, C, C++, Node, etc. You can choose which language to use when implementing the service or client. gRPC also works across multiple languages and platforms, which means you can have your server written in one language and your client written in another language in your application. In our sample, we will develop our client and server in both the Go and Java languages, so you can follow whichever implementation you prefer to use.

In order to generate source code from the service definition, we can either manually compile the proto file using the protocol buffer compiler (*https://oreil.ly/CYEbY*) or we can use build automation tools like Bazel, Maven, or Gradle. Those automation tools already have a set of rules defined to generate the code when building the project. Often it is easier to integrate with an existing build tool to generate the source code of the gRPC service and client.

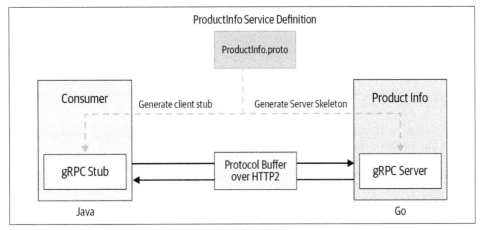

Figure 2-2. A microservice and a consumer based on a service definition

In this sample, we'll use Gradle to build the Java application and use the Gradle protocol buffer plug-in to generate the service and client code. For the Go application, we'll use the protocol buffer compiler and generate the code.

Let's walk through implementing a gRPC server and client in Go and Java. Before we do this, make sure you have installed Java 7 or higher and Go 1.11 or higher on your local machine.

Developing a Service

When you generate the service skeleton code, you will get the low-level code required to establish the gRPC communication, relevant message types, and interfaces. The task of service implementation is all about implementing the interfaces that are generated with the code generation step. Let's start with implementing the Go service and then we will look at how to implement the same service in the Java language.

Implementing a gRPC service with Go

Implementing the Go service has three steps. First, we need to generate the stubs for the service definition, then we implement the business logic of all the remote methods of the service, and finally, we create a server listening on a specified port and register the service to accept client requests. Let's start by creating a new Go module. Here we are going to create one module and a subdirectory inside the module; the module `productinfo/service` is used to keep the service code and the subdirectory (`ecommerce`) is used to keep the autogenerated stub file. Create a directory inside the *productinfo* directory and call it *service*. Navigate inside to the *service* directory and execute the following command to create the module `productinfo/service`:

```
go mod init productinfo/service
```

Once you create the module and create a subdirectory inside the module, you will get a module structure as follows:

```
└ productinfo
        └ service
             ├─ go.mod
             ├ . . .
             └─ ecommerce
                  └ . . .
```

We also need to update the *go.mod* file with the dependencies with the specific version as shown in the following:

```
module productinfo/service

require (
  github.com/gofrs/uuid v3.2.0
  github.com/golang/protobuf v1.3.2
  github.com/google/uuid v1.1.1
  google.golang.org/grpc v1.24.0
)
```

 From Go 1.11 onwards, a new concept called *modules* has been introduced that allows developers to create and build Go projects outside GOPATH. To create a Go module, we need to create a new directory anywhere outside `$GOPATH/src` and inside the directory, we need to execute the command to initialize the module with a module name like the following:

```
go mod init <module_name>
```

Once you initialize the module, a *go.mod* file will be created inside the root of the module. And then we can create our Go source file inside the module and build it. Go resolves imports by using the specific dependency module versions listed in *go.mod*.

Generating client/server stubs.   Now we'll generate client/server stubs manually, using the protocol buffer compiler. To do that, we need to fulfill a set of prerequisites as listed here:

- Download and install the latest protocol buffer version 3 compiler from the GitHub release page (*https://oreil.ly/Ez8qu*).

 When downloading the compiler, you need to choose the compiler that suits your platform. For example, if you are using a 64-bit Linux machine and you need to get a protocol buffer compiler version x.x.x, you need to download the *protoc-x.x.x-linux-x86_64.zip* file.

- Install the gRPC library using the following command:

```
go get -u google.golang.org/grpc
```

- Install the protoc plug-in for Go using the following command:

```
go get -u github.com/golang/protobuf/protoc-gen-go
```

Once we fulfill all the prerequisites, we can generate the code for the service definition by executing the protoc command as shown here:

```
protoc -I ecommerce \ ❶
  ecommerce/product_info.proto \ ❷
  --go_out=plugins=grpc:<module_dir_path>/ecommerce ❸
```

❶   Specifies the directory path where the source proto file and dependent proto files exist (specified with the `--proto_path` or `-I` command-line flag). If you do not specify a value, the current directory is used as the source directory. Inside the directory, we need to arrange the dependent proto files in accordance with the package name.

❷   Specifies the proto file path you want to compile. The compiler will read the file and generate the output Go file.

❸   Specifies the destination directory where you want the generated code to go.

When we execute the command, a stub file (*product_info.pb.go*) will be generated inside the given subdirectory (*ecommerce*) in the module. Now that we have generated the stubs, we need to implement our business logic using the generated code.

Implementing business logic. First, let's create a new Go file named *productinfo_service.go* inside the Go module (`productinfo/service`) and implement the remote methods as shown in Example 2-6.

Example 2-6. gRPC service implementation of ProductInfo service in Go

```go
package main

import (
  "context"
  "errors"
  "log"

  "github.com/gofrs/uuid"
  pb "productinfo/service/ecommerce"   ❶

)

// server is used to implement ecommerce/product_info.
type server struct{   ❷
  productMap map[string]*pb.Product
}

// AddProduct implements ecommerce.AddProduct
func (s *server) AddProduct(ctx context.Context,
                       in *pb.Product) (*pb.ProductID, error) {   ❸❺❻
  out, err := uuid.NewV4()
  if err != nil {
     return nil, status.Errorf(codes.Internal,
         "Error while generating Product ID", err)
  }
  in.Id = out.String()
  if s.productMap == nil {
     s.productMap = make(map[string]*pb.Product)
  }
  s.productMap[in.Id] = in
  return &pb.ProductID{Value: in.Id}, status.New(codes.OK, "").Err()

}

// GetProduct implements ecommerce.GetProduct
func (s *server) GetProduct(ctx context.Context, in *pb.ProductID)
                          (*pb.Product, error) {   ❹❺❻
  value, exists := s.productMap[in.Value]
  if exists {
    return value, status.New(codes.OK, "").Err()
  }
  return nil, status.Errorf(codes.NotFound, "Product does not exist.", in.Value)

}
```

❶ Import the package that contains the generated code we just created from the protobuf compiler.

❷ The `server` struct is an abstraction of the server. It allows attaching service methods to the server.

❸ The `AddProduct` method takes `Product` as a parameter and returns a `ProductID`. `Product` and `ProductID` structs are defined in the *product_info.pb.go* file, which is autogenerated from the *product_info.proto* definition.

❹ The `GetProduct` method takes `ProductID` as a parameter and returns a `Product`.

❺ Both methods also have a `Context` parameter. A `Context` object contains metadata such as the identity of the end user authorization tokens and the request's deadline, and it will exist during the lifetime of the request.

❻ Both methods return an error in addition to the return value of the remote method (methods have multiple return types). These errors are propagated to the consumers and can be used for error handling at the consumer side.

That's all you have to do to implement the business logic of the `ProductInfo` service. Then we can create a simple server that hosts the service and accepts requests from the client.

Creating a Go server.   To create the server in Go, let's create a new Go file named *main.go* inside the same Go package (`productinfo/service`) and implement the `main` method as shown in Example 2-7.

Example 2-7. gRPC server implementation to host ProductInfo service in Go

```go
package main

import (
    "log"
    "net"

    pb "productinfo/service/ecommerce" ❶
    "google.golang.org/grpc"
)

const (
    port = ":50051"
)

func main() {
    lis, err := net.Listen("tcp", port) ❷
```

```
  if err != nil {
    log.Fatalf("failed to listen: %v", err)
  }
  s := grpc.NewServer() ❸
  pb.RegisterProductInfoServer(s, &server{}) ❹

  log.Printf("Starting gRPC listener on port " + port)
  if err := s.Serve(lis); err != nil { ❺
    log.Fatalf("failed to serve: %v", err)
  }
}
```

❶ Import the package that contains the generated code we just created from the protobuf compiler.

❷ TCP listener that we want the gRPC server to bind to is created on the port (50051).

❸ New gRPC server instance is created by calling gRPC Go APIs.

❹ The service implemented earlier is registered to the newly created gRPC server by calling generated APIs.

❺ Start listening to the incoming messages on the port (50051).

Now we have completed building a gRPC service for our business use case in the Go language. And also we created a simple server that will expose service methods and accept messages from gRPC clients.

If you prefer using Java for building a service, we can implement the same service using Java. The implementation procedure is quite similar to Go. So, let's create the same service using the Java language. However, if you are interested in building a client application in Go instead, go directly to "Developing a gRPC Client" on page 36.

Implementing a gRPC Service with Java

When creating a Java gRPC project, the best approach is to use an existing build tool like Gradle, Maven, or Bazel because it manages all dependencies and code generation, etc. In our sample, we will use Gradle to manage the project and we'll discuss how to create a Java project using Gradle and how to implement the business logic of all remote methods of the service. Finally, we'll create a server and register the service to accept client requests.

Gradle is a build automation tool that supports multiple languages, including Java, Scala, Android, C/C++, and Groovy, and is closely integrated with development tools like Eclipse and IntelliJ IDEA. You can install Gradle on your machine by following the steps given on the official page (*https://gradle.org/install*).

Setting up a Java project. Let's first create a Gradle Java project (`product-info-service`). Once you have then created the project, you will get a project structure like the following:

```
product-info-service

├── build.gradle
├ . . .
└── src
    ├── main
    │   ├── java
    │   └── resources
    └── test
        ├── java
        └── resources
```

Under the *src/main* directory, create a *proto* directory and add our `ProductInfo` service definition file (*.proto* file) inside the *proto* directory.

Next, you need to update the *build.gradle* file and add dependencies and the protobuf plug-in for Gradle. Update the *build.gradle* file as shown in Example 2-8.

Example 2-8. Gradle configuration for gRPC Java project

```
apply plugin: 'java'
apply plugin: 'com.google.protobuf'

repositories {
    mavenCentral()
}


def grpcVersion = '1.24.1'  ❶

dependencies {  ❷
    compile "io.grpc:grpc-netty:${grpcVersion}"
    compile "io.grpc:grpc-protobuf:${grpcVersion}"
    compile "io.grpc:grpc-stub:${grpcVersion}"
    compile 'com.google.protobuf:protobuf-java:3.9.2'
}

buildscript {
    repositories {
```

```
        mavenCentral()
    }
    dependencies { ❸

        classpath 'com.google.protobuf:protobuf-gradle-plugin:0.8.10'
    }
}

protobuf { ❹
    protoc {
        artifact = 'com.google.protobuf:protoc:3.9.2'
    }
    plugins {
        grpc {
            artifact = "io.grpc:protoc-gen-grpc-java:${grpcVersion}"
        }
    }
    generateProtoTasks {
        all()*.plugins {
            grpc {}
        }
    }
}

sourceSets { ❺
    main {
        java {
            srcDirs 'build/generated/source/proto/main/grpc'
            srcDirs 'build/generated/source/proto/main/java'
        }
    }
}

jar { ❻
    manifest {
        attributes "Main-Class": "ecommerce.ProductInfoServer"
    }
    from {
        configurations.compile.collect { it.isDirectory() ? it : zipTree(it) }
    }
}

apply plugin: 'application'

startScripts.enabled = false
```

❶   gRPC Java library version used in the Gradle project.

❷   External dependencies we need to use in this project.

❸ Gradle protobuf plug-in version we are using in the project. Use plug-in version 0.7.5 if your Gradle version is lower than 2.12.

❹ In the protobuf plug-in, we need to specify the protobuf compiler version and protobuf Java executable version.

❺ This is to inform IDEs like IntelliJ IDEA, Eclipse, or NetBeans about the generated code.

❻ Configure the main class to use when running the application.

Then run the following command to build the library and generate stub code from the protobuf build plug-in:

```
$ ./gradle build
```

Now we have the Java project ready with autogenerated code. Let's implement the service interface and add business logic to the remote methods.

Implementing business logic.   To start with, let's create the Java package (ecommerce) inside the *src/main/java* source directory and create a Java class (*ProductInfoImpl.java*) inside the package. Then we'll implement the remote methods as shown in Example 2-9.

Example 2-9. gRPC service implementation of ProductInfo service in Java

```
package ecommerce;

import io.grpc.Status;
import io.grpc.StatusException;

import java.util.HashMap;
import java.util.Map;
import java.util.UUID;

public class ProductInfoImpl extends ProductInfoGrpc.ProductInfoImplBase { ❶

    private Map productMap = new HashMap<String, ProductInfoOuterClass.Product>();

    @Override
    public void addProduct(
        ProductInfoOuterClass.Product request,
        io.grpc.stub.StreamObserver
            <ProductInfoOuterClass.ProductID> responseObserver ) { ❷❸
        UUID uuid = UUID.randomUUID();
        String randomUUIDString = uuid.toString();
        productMap.put(randomUUIDString, request);
        ProductInfoOuterClass.ProductID id =
            ProductInfoOuterClass.ProductID.newBuilder()
```

```
                .setValue(randomUUIDString).build();
            responseObserver.onNext(id); ❺
            responseObserver.onCompleted(); ❻
        }

    @Override
    public void getProduct(
        ProductInfoOuterClass.ProductID request,
        io.grpc.stub.StreamObserver
            <ProductInfoOuterClass.Product> responseObserver ) { ❸❹
        String id = request.getValue();
        if (productMap.containsKey(id)) {
            responseObserver.onNext(
                (ProductInfoOuterClass.Product) productMap.get(id)); ❺
            responseObserver.onCompleted(); ❻
        } else {
            responseObserver.onError(new StatusException(Status.NOT_FOUND)); ❼
        }
    }
}
```

❶ Extend the abstract class (ProductInfoGrpc.ProductInfoImplBase) that is gen-
    erated from the plug-in. This will allow adding business logic to AddProduct and
    GetProduct methods defined in the service definition.

❷ The AddProduct method takes Product(ProductInfoOuterClass.Product) as a
    parameter. The Product class is defined in the ProductInfoOuterClass class,
    which is generated from the service definition.

❸ The GetProduct method takes ProductID(ProductInfoOuterClass.ProductID)
    as a parameter. The ProductID class is defined in the ProductInfoOuterClass
    class, which is generated from the service definition.

❹ The responseObserver object is used to send the response back to the client and
    close the stream.

❺ Send a response back to the client.

❻ End the client call by closing the stream.

❼ Send an error back to the client.

That's all you need to do to implement the business logic of the ProductInfo service
in Java. Then we can create a simple server that hosts the service and accepts requests
from the client.

Creating a Java server. In order to expose our service to the outside, we need to create a gRPC server instance and register our `ProductInfo` service to the server. The server will listen on the specified port and dispatch all requests to the relevant service. Let's create a main class (*ProductInfoServer.java*) inside the package as shown in Example 2-10.

Example 2-10. gRPC server implementation to host ProductInfo service in Java

```java
package ecommerce;

import io.grpc.Server;
import io.grpc.ServerBuilder;

import java.io.IOException;

public class ProductInfoServer {

    public static void main(String[] args)
            throws IOException, InterruptedException {
        int port = 50051;
        Server server = ServerBuilder.forPort(port)     ❶
                .addService(new ProductInfoImpl())
                .build()
                .start();
        System.out.println("Server started, listening on " + port);
        Runtime.getRuntime().addShutdownHook(new Thread(() -> {   ❷
            System.err.println("Shutting down gRPC server since JVM is " +
                "shutting down");
            if (server != null) {
                server.shutdown();
            }
            System.err.println("Server shut down");
        }));
        server.awaitTermination();     ❸
    }
}
```

❶ Server instance is created on port 50051. This is the port we want the server to bind to and where it will listen to incoming messages. Our `ProductInfo` service implementation is added to the server.

❷ A runtime shutdown hook is added to shut down the gRPC server when JVM shuts down.

❸ At the end of the method, the server thread is held until the server gets terminated.

Now we are done with the implementation of the gRPC service in both languages. We can then proceed to the implementation of the gRPC client.

Developing a gRPC Client

As we did with the gRPC service implementation, we can now discuss how to create an application to talk with the server. Let's start off with the generation of the client-side stubs from the service definition. On top of the generated client stub, we can create a simple gRPC client to connect with our gRPC server and invoke the remote methods that it offers.

In this sample, we are going to write client applications in both the Java and Go languages. But you don't need to create your server and client in the same language, or run them on the same platform. Since gRPC works across languages and platforms, you can create them in any supported language. Let's discuss the Go implementation first. If you are interested in the Java implementation, you may skip the next section and go directly into the Java client.

Implementing a gRPC Go client

Let's start by creating a new Go module (`productinfo/client`) and subdirectory (*ecommerce*) inside the module. In order to implement the Go client application, we also need to generate the stub as we have done when implementing the Go service. Since we need to create the same file (*product_info.pb.go*) and need to follow the same steps to generate the stubs, we are not going to mention it here. Please refer to "Generating client/server stubs" on page 27 to generate stub files.

Let's create a new Go file named *productinfo_client.go* inside the Go module (`produc tinfo/client`) and implement the main method to invoke remote methods as shown in Example 2-11.

Example 2-11. gRPC client application in Go

```
package main

import (
  "context"
  "log"
  "time"

  pb "productinfo/client/ecommerce" ❶
  "google.golang.org/grpc"
)

const (
  address = "localhost:50051"
```

```
)

func main() {

  conn, err := grpc.Dial(address, grpc.WithInsecure()) ❷
  if err != nil {
    log.Fatalf("did not connect: %v", err)
  }
  defer conn.Close() ❼
  c := pb.NewProductInfoClient(conn) ❸

  name := "Apple iPhone 11"
  description := `Meet Apple iPhone 11. All-new dual-camera system with
             Ultra Wide and Night mode.`
  price := float32(1000.0)
  ctx, cancel := context.WithTimeout(context.Background(), time.Second) ❹
  defer cancel()
  r, err := c.AddProduct(ctx,
        &pb.Product{Name: name, Description: description, Price: price}) ❺
  if err != nil {
    log.Fatalf("Could not add product: %v", err)
  }
  log.Printf("Product ID: %s added successfully", r.Value)

  product, err := c.GetProduct(ctx, &pb.ProductID{Value: r.Value}) ❻
  if err != nil {
    log.Fatalf("Could not get product: %v", err)
  }
  log.Printf("Product: ", product.String())

}
```

❶ Import the package that contains the generated code we created from the proto-buf compiler.

❷ Set up a connection with the server from the provided address ("localhost: 50051"). Here we create an unsecured connection between client and server.

❸ Pass the connection and create a stub. This stub instance contains all the remote methods to invoke the server.

❹ Create a Context to pass with the remote call. Here the Context object contains metadata such as the identity of the end user, authorization tokens, and the request's deadline and it will exist during the lifetime of the request.

❺ Call addProduct method with product details. This returns a product ID if the action completed successfully. Otherwise it returns an error.

❻ Call `getProduct` with the product ID. This returns product details if the action completed successfully. Otherwise it returns an error.

❼ Close the connection when everything is done.

Now we have completed building the gRPC client in the Go language. Let's next create a client using the Java language. This is not a mandatory step to follow. If you are also interested in building a gRPC client in Java, you can continue; otherwise, you can skip the next section and go directly to "Building and Running" on page 39.

Implementing a Java client

In order to create a Java client application, we also need to set up a Gradle project (`product-info-client`) and generate classes using the Gradle plug-in as we did when implementing the Java service. Please follow the steps in "Setting up a Java project" on page 31 to set up a Java client project.

Once you generate the client stub code for your project via the Gradle build tool, let's create a new class called `ProductInfoClient` inside the `ecommerce` package and add the content in Example 2-12.

Example 2-12. gRPC client application in Java

```
package ecommerce;

import io.grpc.ManagedChannel;
import io.grpc.ManagedChannelBuilder;

import java.util.logging.Logger;

/**
 * gRPC client sample for productInfo service.
 */
public class ProductInfoClient {

    public static void main(String[] args) throws InterruptedException {
        ManagedChannel channel = ManagedChannelBuilder
            .forAddress("localhost", 50051) ❶
            .usePlaintext()
            .build();

        ProductInfoGrpc.ProductInfoBlockingStub stub =
            ProductInfoGrpc.newBlockingStub(channel); ❷

        ProductInfoOuterClass.ProductID productID = stub.addProduct(   ❸
            ProductInfoOuterClass.Product.newBuilder()
                .setName("Apple iPhone 11")
                .setDescription("Meet Apple iPhone 11. " +
                    All-new dual-camera system with " +
```

```
                            "Ultra Wide and Night mode.");
                    .setPrice(1000.0f)
                    .build());
        System.out.println(productID.getValue());

        ProductInfoOuterClass.Product product = stub.getProduct(productID);  ❹
        System.out.println(product.toString());
        channel.shutdown();  ❺
    }
}
```

❶ Create a gRPC channel specifying the server address and port we want to con-
    nect to. Here we are trying to connect to a server running on the same machine
    and listening on port 50051. We also enable plaintext, which means we are set-
    ting up an unsecured connection between client and server.

❷ Create the client stub using the newly created channel. We can create two types of
    stubs. One is the BlockingStub, which waits until it receives a server response.
    The other one is the NonBlockingStub, which doesn't wait for server response,
    but instead registers an observer to receive the response. In this example, we use
    a BlockingStub to make the client simple.

❸ Call addProduct method using the product details. This returns a product ID if
    the action completed successfully.

❹ Call getProduct with the product ID. Returns the product details if the action
    completed successfully.

❺ Close the connection when everything is done so that the network resources that
    we used in our application are safely returned back after we are finished.

Now we have finished developing the gRPC client. Let's make the client and server
talk to each other.

Building and Running

It's time to build and run the gRPC server and client applications that we have created. You can deploy and run a gRPC application on your local machine, on a virtual
machine, on Docker, or on Kubernetes. In this section, we will discuss how to build
and run the gRPC server and client applications on a local machine.

> We will cover how to deploy and run gRPC applications on Docker
> and Kubernetes environments in Chapter 7.

Let's run the gRPC server and client applications that we have just developed in your local machine. Since our server and client applications are written in two languages, we are going to build the server application separately.

Building a Go Server

When we implement a Go service, the final package structure in the workspace looks like the following:

```
└ productinfo
        └ service
            ├ go.mod
            ├ main.go
            ├ productinfo_service.go
            └ ecommerce
                └ product_info.pb.go
```

We can build our service to generate a service binary (*bin/server*). In order to build, first go to the Go module root directory location (*productinfo/service*) and execute the following shell command:

```
$ go build -i -v -o bin/server
```

Once the build is successful, an executable file (*bin/server*) is created under the *bin* directory.

Next, let's set up the Go client!

Building a Go Client

When we implement a Go client, the package structure in the workspace looks like:

```
└ productinfo
        └ client
            ├ go.mod
            ├main.go
            └ ecommerce
                └ product_info.pb.go
```

We can build the client code the same way we built the Go service using the following shell command:

```
$ go build -i -v -o bin/client
```

Once the build is successful, an executable file (*bin/client*) is created under the *bin* directory. The next step is to run the files!

Running a Go Server and Client

We've just built a client and a server. Let's run them on separate terminals and make them talk to each other:

```
// Running Server
$ bin/server
2019/08/08 10:17:58 Starting gRPC listener on port :50051

// Running Client
$ bin/client
2019/08/08 11:20:01 Product ID: 5d0e7cdc-b9a0-11e9-93a4-6c96cfe0687d
added successfully
2019/08/08 11:20:01 Product: id:"5d0e7cdc-b9a0-11e9-93a4-6c96cfe0687d"
        name:"Apple iPhone 11"
        description:"Meet Apple iPhone 11. All-new dual-camera system with
        Ultra Wide and Night mode."
        price:1000
```

Next we'll build a Java server.

Building a Java Server

Since we implement the Java service as a Gradle project, we can easily build the project using the following command:

```
$ gradle build
```

Once the build is successful, the executable JAR (*server.jar*) file is created under the *build/libs* directory.

Building a Java Client

Just as with a service, we can easily build the project using the following command:

```
$ gradle build
```

Once the build is successful, the executable JAR (*client.jar*) file is created under the *build/libs* directory.

Running a Java Server and Client

We've now built both a client and server in the Java language. Let's run them:

```
$ java -jar build/libs/server.jar
INFO: Server started, listening on 50051

$ java -jar build/libs/client.jar
INFO: Product ID: a143af20-12e6-483e-a28f-15a38b757ea8 added successfully.
INFO: Product: name: "Apple iPhone 11"
description: "Meet Apple iPhone 11. All-new dual-camera system with
Ultra Wide and Night mode."
price: 1000.0
```

Now we have built and run our sample successfully on local machines. Once we successfully run the client and server, the client application first invokes the addProduct method with product details and receives the product identifier of the newly added product as the response. Then it retrieves the newly added product details by calling the getProduct method with the product identifier. As we mentioned earlier in this chapter, we don't need to write the client in the same language to talk with the server. We can run a gRPC Java server and Go client and it will work without any issue.

That brings us to the end of the chapter!

Summary

When you develop a gRPC application, you first define a service interface definition using protocol buffers, a language-agnostic, platform-neutral, extensible mechanism for serializing structured data. Next, you generate server-side and client-side code for the programming language of your choice, which simplifies the server- and client-side logic by providing the low-level communication abstractions. From the server side, you implement the logic of the method that you expose remotely and run a gRPC server that binds the service. On the client side, you connect to the remote gRPC server and invoke the remote method using the generated client-side code.

This chapter is mainly about getting hands-on experience with developing and running gRPC server and client applications. The experience you gain by following the session is quite useful when building a real-world gRPC application because irrespective of which language you are using, you need similar steps to build a gRPC application. So, in the next chapter, we will further extend the concepts and technologies you learned to build real-world use cases.

gRPC Communication Patterns

In the first couple of chapters, you learned the basics of gRPC's inter-process communication techniques and got some hands-on experience in building a simple gRPC-based application. So far what we have done is define a service interface, implement a service, run a gRPC server, and invoke service operations remotely through a gRPC client application. The communication pattern between the client and the server is a simple request–response style communication, where you get a single response for a single request. However, with gRPC, you can leverage different inter-process communication patterns (or RPC styles) other than the simple request–response pattern.

In this chapter, we'll explore four fundamental communication patterns used in gRPC-based applications: unary RPC (simple RPC), server-side streaming, client-side streaming, and bidirectional streaming. We'll use some real-world use cases to showcase each pattern, define a service definition using a gRPC IDL, and implement both the service and client side using Go.

Go and Java Code Samples

To maintain consistency, all the code samples in this chapter are written using Go. But if you are a Java developer, you can also find the complete Java code samples for the same use cases in the source code repository for this book.

Simple RPC (Unary RPC)

Let's begin our discussion on gRPC communication patterns with the simplest RPC style, *simple RPC*, which is also known as *unary RPC*. In simple RPC, when a client invokes a remote function of a server, the client sends a single request to the server and gets a single response that is sent along with status details and trailing metadata. In fact, this is exactly the same communication pattern that you learned in Chapters 1 and 2. Let's try to understand the simple RPC pattern further with a real-world use case.

Suppose we need to build an OrderManagement service for an online retail application based on gRPC. One of the methods that we have to implement as part of this service is a getOrder method, where the client can retrieve an existing order by providing the order ID. As shown in Figure 3-1, the client is sending a single request with the order ID and the service responds with a single response that contains the order information. Hence, it follows the simple RPC pattern.

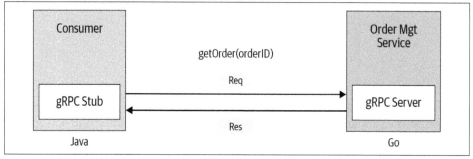

Figure 3-1. Simple/unary RPC

Now let's proceed to the implementation of this pattern. The first step is to create the service definition for the OrderManagement service with the getOrder method. As shown in the code snippet in Example 3-1, we can define the service definition using protocol buffers, and the getOrder remote method takes a single request order ID and responds with a single response, which comprises the Order message. The Order message has the required structure to represent the order in this use case.

Example 3-1. Service definition of OrderManagement with getOrder method that uses simple RPC pattern

```
syntax = "proto3";

import "google/protobuf/wrappers.proto"; ❶

package ecommerce;

service OrderManagement {
    rpc getOrder(google.protobuf.StringValue) returns (Order); ❷
}

message Order { ❸
    string id = 1;
    repeated string items = 2; ❹
    string description = 3;
    float price = 4;
```

```
    string destination = 5;
}
```

❶ Use this package to leverage the well-known types such as StringValue.

❷ Remote method for retrieving an order.

❸ Define the Order type.

❹ repeated is used to represent the fields that can be repeated any number of times including zero in a message. Here one order message can have any number of items.

Then, using the gRPC service definition proto file, you can generate the server skeleton code and implement the logic of the getOrder method. In the code snippet in Example 3-2, what we have shown is the Go implementation of the OrderManagement service. As the input of the getOrder method, you get a single order ID (String) as the request and you can simply find the order from the server side and respond with an Order message (Order struct). The Order message can be returned along with a nil error to tell gRPC that we've finished dealing with the RPC and the Order can be returned to the client.

Example 3-2. Service implementation of OrderManagement with getOrder in Go

```
// server/main.go
func (s *server) GetOrder(ctx context.Context,
        orderId *wrapper.StringValue) (*pb.Order, error) {
    // Service Implementation.
        ord := orderMap[orderId.Value]
        return &ord, nil
}
```

 The low-level details of the complete message flow of a gRPC server and client are explained in Chapter 4. In addition to the method parameters that we have specified for the getOrder method in your service definition, you can observe that there is another Context parameter passed to the method in the preceding Go implementation of the OrderManagement service. Context carries some of the constructs such as deadlines and cancellations that are used to control gRPC behavior. We'll discuss those concepts in detail in Chapter 5.

Now let's implement the client-side logic to invoke the getOrder method remotely. As with the server-side implementation, you can generate code for the preferred language to create the client-side stub and then use that stub to invoke the service. In

Example 3-3, we have used a Go gRPC client to invoke the OrderManagement service. The first steps, of course, are to set up the connection to the server and initiate the client stub to invoke the service. Then you can simply invoke the client stub's getOr der method to invoke the remote method. As the response, you get an Order message that contains the order information that we define using protocol buffers in our service definition.

Example 3-3. Client implementation to invoke remote method getOrder using Go

```
// Setting up a connection to the server.
...
orderMgtClient := pb.NewOrderManagementClient(conn)
...

// Get Order
retrievedOrder , err := orderMgtClient.GetOrder(ctx,
        &wrapper.StringValue{Value: "106"})
log.Print("GetOrder Response -> : ", retrievedOrder)
```

The simple RPC pattern is quite straightforward to implement and fits well for most inter-process communication use cases. The implementation is quite similar across multiple programming languages, and you can find the source code for Go and Java in the sample source code repository of the book.

Now, since you have a good understanding of the simple RPC communication pattern, let's move on to *server-streaming RPC*.

Server-Streaming RPC

In simple RPC you always had a single request and single response in the communication between the gRPC server and gRPC client. In server-side streaming RPC, the server sends back a sequence of responses after getting the client's request message. This sequence of multiple responses is known as a "stream." After sending all the server responses, the server marks the end of the stream by sending the server's status details as trailing metadata to the client.

Let's take a real-world use case to understand server-side streaming further. In our OrderManagement service suppose that we need to build an order search capability where we can provide a search term and get the matching results (Figure 3-2). Rather than sending all the matching orders at once, the OrderManagement service can send the orders as and when they are found. This means the order service client will receive multiple response messages for a single request that it has sent.

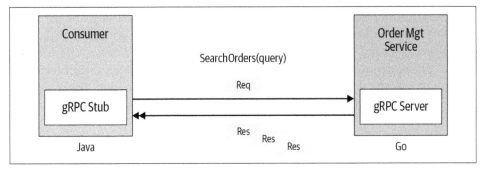

Figure 3-2. Server-streaming RPC

Now let's include a searchOrder method in our gRPC service definition of the Order Management service. As shown in Example 3-4, the method definition is quite similar to simple RPC, but as the return parameter, you have to specify a *stream* of orders by using returns (stream Order) in the proto file of the service definition.

Example 3-4. Service definition with server-side streaming RPC

```
syntax = "proto3";

import "google/protobuf/wrappers.proto";

package ecommerce;

service OrderManagement {
    ...
    rpc searchOrders(google.protobuf.StringValue) returns (stream Order); ❶
    ...
}

message Order {
    string id = 1;
    repeated string items = 2;
    string description = 3;
    float price = 4;
    string destination = 5;
}
```

❶ Defining server-side streaming by returning a stream of Order messages.

From the service definition, you can generate the server-side code and then by implementing the generated interfaces you build the logic of the searchOrder method of the OrderManagement gRPC service. In the Go implementation shown in Example 3-5, the SearchOrders method has two parameters: searchQuery, a string value, and a special parameter OrderManagement_SearchOrdersServer to write our responses to. `OrderManagement_SearchOrdersServer` acts as a reference object to the stream that we can write multiple responses to. The business logic here is to find the matching orders and send them one by one via the stream. When a new order is found, it is written to the stream using the `Send(…)` method of the stream reference object. Once all the responses are written to the stream you can mark the end of the stream by returning `nil`, and the server status and other trailing metadata will be sent to the client.

Example 3-5. Service implementation of OrderManagement with searchOrders in Go

```go
func (s *server) SearchOrders(searchQuery *wrappers.StringValue,
        stream pb.OrderManagement_SearchOrdersServer) error {

    for key, order := range orderMap {
        log.Print(key, order)
        for _, itemStr := range order.Items {
            log.Print(itemStr)
            if strings.Contains(
                    itemStr, searchQuery.Value) { ❶
                // Send the matching orders in a stream
                err := stream.Send(&order) ❷
                if err != nil {
                    return fmt.Errorf(
                            "error sending message to stream : %v",
                            err) ❸
                }
                log.Print("Matching Order Found : " + key)
                break
            }
        }
    }
    return nil
}
```

❶ Find matching orders.

❷ Send matching order through the stream.

❸ Check for possible errors that could occur when streaming messages to the client.

The remote method invocation from the client side is quite similar to simple RPC. However, here you have to process multiple responses as the server writes multiple responses to the stream. So in the Go implementation of the gRPC client (Example 3-6), we retrieve messages from the client-side stream using the `Recv()` method and keep doing so until we reach the end of the stream.

Example 3-6. Client implementation of OrderManagement with searchOrders in Go

```
// Setting up a connection to the server.
...
      c := pb.NewOrderManagementClient(conn)
...
    searchStream, _ := c.SearchOrders(ctx,
        &wrapper.StringValue{Value: "Google"}) ❶

      for {
              searchOrder, err := searchStream.Recv() ❷
              if err == io.EOF { ❸
                    break
              }
        // handle other possible errors
              log.Print("Search Result : ", searchOrder)
      }
```

❶ The SearchOrders function returns a client stream of OrderManagement_Search
OrdersClient, which has a Recv method.

❷ Calling the client stream's Recv() method to retrieve Order responses one by one.

❸ When the end of the stream is found Recv returns an io.EOF.

Now let's look at client-streaming RPC, which is pretty much the opposite of server-streaming RPC.

Client-Streaming RPC

In client-streaming RPC, the client sends multiple messages to the server instead of a single request. The server sends back a single response to the client. However, the server does not necessarily have to wait until it receives all the messages from the client side to send a response. Based on this logic you may send the response after reading one or a few messages from the stream or after reading all the messages.

Let's further extend our OrderManagement service to understand client-streaming RPC. Suppose you want to include a new method, updateOrders, in the OrderManage ment service to update a set of orders (Figure 3-3). Here we want to send the order list as a stream of messages to the server and server will process that stream and send a message with the status of the orders that are updated.

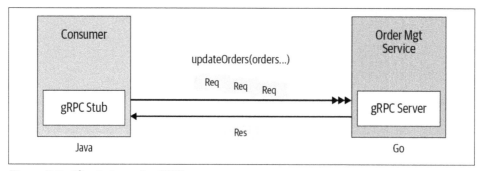

Figure 3-3. Client-streaming RPC

Then we can include the `updateOrders` method in our service definition of the `Order Management` service as shown in Example 3-7. You can simply use `stream order` as the method parameter of `updateOrders` to denote that `updateOrders` will get multiple messages as the input from the client. As the server only sends a single response, the return value is a single string message.

Example 3-7. Service definition with client-side streaming RPC

```
syntax = "proto3";

import "google/protobuf/wrappers.proto";

package ecommerce;

service OrderManagement {
...
    rpc updateOrders(stream Order) returns (google.protobuf.StringValue);
...
}

message Order {
    string id = 1;
    repeated string items = 2;
    string description = 3;
    float price = 4;
    string destination = 5;
}
```

Once we update the service definition, we can generate the server- and client-side code. At the server side, you need to implement the generated method interface of the `UpdateOrders` method of the `OrderManagement` service. In the Go implementation shown in Example 3-8, `UpdateOrders` has an `OrderManagement_UpdateOrdersServer` parameter, which is the reference object to the incoming message stream from the client. Therefore, you can read messages via that object by calling the `Recv()` method.

Depending on the business logic, you may read a few messages or all the messages until the end of the stream. The service can send its response simply by calling the `SendAndClose` method of the `OrderManagement_UpdateOrdersServer` object, which also marks the end of the stream for server-side messages. If the server decides to prematurely stop reading from the client's stream, the server should cancel the client stream so the client knows to stop producing messages.

Example 3-8. Service implementation of OrderManagement with updateOrders method in Go

```go
func (s *server) UpdateOrders(stream pb.OrderManagement_UpdateOrdersServer) error {

        ordersStr := "Updated Order IDs : "
        for {
                order, err := stream.Recv() ❶
                if err == io.EOF { ❷
                        // Finished reading the order stream.
                        return stream.SendAndClose(
                                &wrapper.StringValue{Value: "Orders processed "
                                + ordersStr})
                }
                // Update order
                orderMap[order.Id] = *order

                log.Printf("Order ID ", order.Id, ": Updated")
                ordersStr += order.Id + ", "
        }
}
```

❶ Read message from the client stream.

❷ Check for end of stream.

Now let's look at the client-side implementation of the client-streaming RPC use case. As shown in the following Go implementation (Example 3-9), the client can send multiple messages via the client-side stream reference using the `updateStream.Send` method. Once all the messages are streamed the client can mark the end of the stream and receive the response from the service. This is done using the `CloseAndRecv` method of the stream reference.

Example 3-9. Client implementation of OrderManagement with updateOrders method in Go

```go
// Setting up a connection to the server.
...
        c := pb.NewOrderManagementClient(conn)
...
```

```
updateStream, err := client.UpdateOrders(ctx) ❶

    if err != nil { ❷
            log.Fatalf("%v.UpdateOrders(_) = _, %v", client, err)
    }

    // Updating order 1
    if err := updateStream.Send(&updOrder1); err != nil { ❸
            log.Fatalf("%v.Send(%v) = %v",
                    updateStream, updOrder1, err) ❹
    }

    // Updating order 2
    if err := updateStream.Send(&updOrder2); err != nil {
            log.Fatalf("%v.Send(%v) = %v",
                    updateStream, updOrder2, err)
    }

    // Updating order 3
    if err := updateStream.Send(&updOrder3); err != nil {
            log.Fatalf("%v.Send(%v) = %v",
                    updateStream, updOrder3, err)
    }

    updateRes, err := updateStream.CloseAndRecv() ❺
    if err != nil {
            log.Fatalf("%v.CloseAndRecv() got error %v, want %v",
                    updateStream, err, nil)
    }
    log.Printf("Update Orders Res : %s", updateRes)
```

❶ Invoking `UpdateOrders` remote method.

❷ Handling errors related to `UpdateOrders`.

❸ Sending order update via client stream.

❹ Handling errors when sending messages to stream.

❺ Closing the stream and receiving the response.

As a result of this function invocation, you get the response message of the service. Since now you have a good understanding of both server-streaming and client-streaming RPC, let's move on to bidirectional-streaming RPC, which is sort of a combination of the RPC styles that we discussed.

Bidirectional-Streaming RPC

In bidirectional-streaming RPC, the client is sending a request to the server as a stream of messages. The server also responds with a stream of messages. The call has to be initiated from the client side, but after that, the communication is completely based on the application logic of the gRPC client and the server. Let's look at an example to understand bidirectional-streaming RPC in detail. As illustrated in Figure 3-4, in our OrderManagement service use case, suppose we need order processing functionality where you can send a continuous set of orders (the stream of orders) and process them into combined shipments based on the delivery location (i.e., orders are organized into shipments based on the delivery destination).

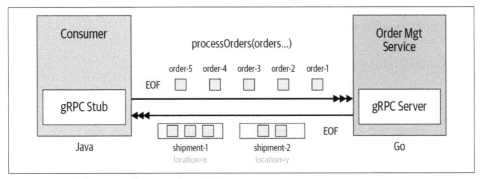

Figure 3-4. Bidirectional-streaming RPC

We can identify the following key steps of this business use case:

- The client application initiates the business use case by setting up the connection with the server and sending call metadata (headers).

- Once the connection setup is completed, the client application sends a continuous set of order IDs that need to be processed by the OrderManagement service.

- Each order ID is sent to the server as a separate gRPC message.

- The service processes each order for the specified order ID and organizes them into combined shipments based on the delivery location of the order.

- A combined shipment may contain multiple orders that should be delivered to the same destination.

- Orders are processed in batches. When the batch size is reached, all the currently created combined shipments will be sent back to the client.

- For example, an ordered stream of four where two orders addressed to location X and two to location Y can be denoted as X, Y, X, Y. And if the batch size is three, then the created combined orders should be shipment [X, X], shipment [Y], shipment [Y]. These combined shipments are also sent as a stream back to the client.

The key idea behind this business use case is that once the RPC method is invoked either the client or service can send messages at any arbitrary time. (This also includes the end of stream markings from either of the parties.)

Now, let's move on to the service definition for the preceding use case. As shown in Example 3-10, we can define a processOrders method so that it takes a stream of strings as the method parameter to represent the order ID stream and a stream of CombinedShipments as the return parameter of the method. So, by declaring both the method parameter and return parameters as a stream, you can define a bidirectional-streaming RPC method. The combined shipment message is also declared in the service definition and it contains a list of order elements.

Example 3-10. Service definition for bidirectional-streaming RPC

```proto
syntax = "proto3";

import "google/protobuf/wrappers.proto";

package ecommerce;

service OrderManagement {
    ...
    rpc processOrders(stream google.protobuf.StringValue)
        returns (stream CombinedShipment); ❶
}

message Order { ❷
    string id = 1;
    repeated string items = 2;
    string description = 3;
    float price = 4;
    string destination = 5;
}

message CombinedShipment { ❸
    string id = 1;
    string status = 2;
    repeated Order ordersList = 3;
}
```

❶ Both method parameters and return parameters are declared as streams in bidirectional RPC.

❷ Structure of the Order message.

❸ Structure of the CombinedShipment message.

Then we can generate the server-side code from the updated service definition. The service should implement the processOrders method of the OrderManagement service. In the Go implementation shown in Example 3-11, processOrders has an Order Management_ProcessOrdersServer parameter, which is the reference object to the message stream between the client and the service. Using this stream object, the service can read the client's messages that are streamed to the server as well as write the stream server's messages back to the client. Using that stream reference object, the incoming message stream can be read using the Recv() method. In the processOr ders method, the service can keep on reading the incoming message stream while writing to the same stream using Send.

To simplify the demonstration, some of the logic of Example 3-10 is not shown. You can find the full code example in this book's source code repository.

Example 3-11. Service implementation of OrderManagement with processOrders method in Go

```go
func (s *server) ProcessOrders(
        stream pb.OrderManagement_ProcessOrdersServer) error {
    ...
    for {
            orderId, err := stream.Recv()    ❶
            if err == io.EOF {               ❷
                    ...
                    for _, comb := range combinedShipmentMap {
                            stream.Send(&comb)    ❸
                    }
                    return nil                    ❹
            }
            if err != nil {
                    return err
            }

            // Logic to organize orders into shipments,
            // based on the destination.
            ...
            //

            if batchMarker == orderBatchSize {    ❺
                    // Stream combined orders to the client in batches
                    for _, comb := range combinedShipmentMap {
                            // Send combined shipment to the client
                            stream.Send(&comb)        ❻
```

```
        }
        batchMarker = 0
        combinedShipmentMap = make(
                map[string]pb.CombinedShipment)
    } else {
        batchMarker++
    }
  }
}
```

❶ Read order IDs from the incoming stream.

❷ Keep reading until the end of the stream is found.

❸ When the end of the stream is found send all the remaining combined shipments to the client.

❹ Server-side end of the stream is marked by returning nil.

❺ Orders are processed in batches. When the batch size is met, all the created combined shipments are streamed to the client.

❻ Writing the combined shipment to the stream.

Here we process incoming orders based on the ID, and when a new combined shipment is created the service writes it to the same stream (unlike client-streaming RPC where we write and close the stream with SendAndClose.). The end of the stream at the server side is marked when we return nil when the client's end of the stream is found.

The client-side implementation (Example 3-12) is also quite similar to the previous examples. When the client invokes the method processOrders via the OrderManagement client object, it gets a reference to the stream (streamProcOrder) that is used in sending messages to the server as well as reading messages from the server.

Example 3-12. Client implementation of OrderManagement with processOrders method in Go

```
// Process Order
streamProcOrder, _ := c.ProcessOrders(ctx) ❶
        if err := streamProcOrder.Send(
                &wrapper.StringValue{Value:"102"}); err != nil { ❷
                log.Fatalf("%v.Send(%v) = %v", client, "102", err)
        }

        if err := streamProcOrder.Send(
                &wrapper.StringValue{Value:"103"}); err != nil {
```

```
                log.Fatalf("%v.Send(%v) = %v", client, "103", err)
        }

        if err := streamProcOrder.Send(
                &wrapper.StringValue{Value:"104"}); err != nil {
                log.Fatalf("%v.Send(%v) = %v", client, "104", err)
        }


        channel := make(chan struct{})   ❸
    go asncClientBidirectionalRPC(streamProcOrder, channel) ❹
    time.Sleep(time.Millisecond * 1000)       ❺

        if err := streamProcOrder.Send(
                &wrapper.StringValue{Value:"101"}); err != nil {
                log.Fatalf("%v.Send(%v) = %v", client, "101", err)
        }

        if err := streamProcOrder.CloseSend(); err != nil { ❻
                log.Fatal(err)
        }

<- channel

func asncClientBidirectionalRPC (
        streamProcOrder pb.OrderManagement_ProcessOrdersClient,
        c chan struct{}) {
    for {
            combinedShipment, errProcOrder := streamProcOrder.Recv() ❼
            if errProcOrder == io.EOF { ❽
                    break
            }
            log.Printf("Combined shipment : ", combinedShipment.OrdersList)
    }
    <-c
}
```

❶ Invoke the remote method and obtain the stream reference for writing and read-
    ing from the client side.

❷ Send a message to the service.

❸ Create a channel to use for Goroutines.

❹ Invoke the function using Goroutines to read the messages in parallel from the
    service.

❺ Mimic a delay when sending some messages to the service.

❻ Mark the end of stream for the client stream (order IDs).

❼ Read service's messages on the client side.

❽ Condition to detect the end of the stream.

The client can send messages to the service and close the stream at any arbitrary time. The same applies for reading as well. In the prior example, we execute the client message writing and message reading logic in two concurrent threads using the Go language's *Goroutines* terminology.

Goroutines

In Go, Goroutines are functions or methods that run concurrently with other functions or methods. They can be thought of as lightweight threads.

So, the client can read and write to the same stream concurrently and both incoming and outgoing streams operate independently. What we have shown is a somewhat complex use case to showcase the power of bidirectional RPC. It's important to understand that the client and server can read and write in any order—the streams operate completely independently. Therefore, it is completely up to the client and service to decide the communication pattern between the client and service once the initial connection is established.

With that, we have covered all the possible communication patterns that we can use to build interactions with gRPC-based applications. There is no hard-and-fast rule when it comes to selecting a communication pattern, but it's always good to analyze the business use case and then select the most appropriate pattern.

Before we conclude this discussion on gRPC communication patterns, it's important to take a look at how gRPC is used for microservices communication.

Using gRPC for Microservices Communication

One of the main usages of gRPC is to implement microservices and their inter-service communication. In microservices inter-service communication, gRPC is used along with other communication protocols and usually gRPC services are implemented as polyglot services (implemented with different programming languages). To understand this further, let's take a real-world scenario (Figure 3-5) of an online retail system, which is an extended version of what we have discussed so far.

In this scenario, we have a number of microservices serving specific business capabilities of the online relation system. There are services such as the Product service, which is implemented as a gRPC service, and there are composite services such as the Catalog service, which calls multiple downstream services to build its business capability. As we discussed in Chapter 1, for most of the synchronous message passing scenarios, we can use gRPC. When you have certain asynchronous messaging scenarios that may require persistent messaging, then you can use event brokers or message brokers, such as Kafka (*https://kafka.apache.org*), Active MQ (*https://activemq.apache.org*), RabbitMQ (*https://www.rabbitmq.com*), and NATS (*http://nats.io*). When you have to expose certain business functionalities to the external world, then you can use the conventional REST/OpenAPI-based services or the GraphQL service. Thus services such as Catalog and Checkout are consuming gRPC-based backend services, and also exposing RESTful or GraphQL-based external-facing interfaces.

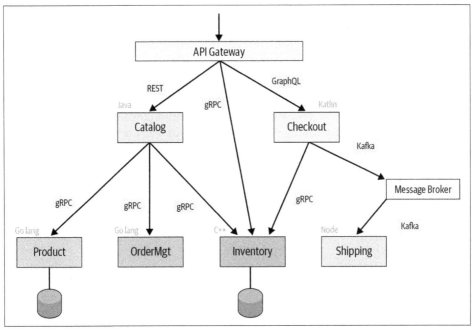

Figure 3-5. A common microservices deployment pattern with gRPC and other protocols

In most of the real-world use cases, these external-facing services are exposed through an API gateway. That is the place where you apply various nonfunctional capabilities such as security, throttling, versioning, and so on. Most such APIs leverage protocols such as REST or GraphQL. Although it's not very common, you may also expose gRPC as an external-facing service, as long as the API gateway supports exposing gRPC interfaces. The API gateway implements cross-cutting functionality such as authentication, logging, versioning, throttling, and load balancing. By using an API gateway with your gRPC APIs, you are able to deploy this functionality outside of your core gRPC services. One of the other important aspects of this architecture is that we can leverage multiple programming languages but share the same service contract between then (i.e., code generation from the same gRPC service definition). This allows us to pick the appropriate implementation technology based on the business capability of the service.

Summary

gRPC offers a diverse set of RPC communication styles for building inter-process communication between gRPC-based applications. In this chapter, we explored four main communication patterns. Simple RPC is the most basic one; it is pretty much a simple request–response style remote procedure invocation. Server-streaming RPC allows you to send multiple messages from the service to the consumer after the first invocation of the remote method, while client streaming allows you to send multiple messages from the client to the service. We delve into the details of how we can implement each of these patterns using some real-world use cases.

The knowledge you gained in this chapter is quite useful for implementing any gRPC use case so that you can select the most appropriate communication pattern for your business. While this chapter gave you a solid understanding of gRPC communication patterns, the low-level communication details that are transparent to the user were not covered in this chapter. In the next chapter, we will dive deep into how low-level communication takes place when we have gRPC-based inter-process communication.

gRPC: Under the Hood

As you have learned in previous chapters, gRPC applications communicate using RPC over the network. As a gRPC application developer, you don't need to worry about the underlying details of how RPC is implemented, what message-encoding techniques are used, and how RPC works over the network. You use the service definition to generate either server- or client-side code for the language of your choice. All the low-level communication details are implemented in the generated code and you get some high-level abstractions to work with. However, when building complex gRPC-based systems and running them in production, it's vital to know how gRPC works under the hood.

In this chapter, we'll explore how the gRPC communication flow is implemented, what encoding techniques are used, how gRPC uses the underlying network communication techniques, and so on. We'll walk you through the message flow where the client invokes a given RPC, then discuss how it gets marshaled to a gRPC call that goes over the network, how the network communication protocol is used, how it is unmarshaled at the server, how the corresponding service and remote function is invoked, and so on.

We'll also look at how we use protocol buffers as the encoding technique and HTTP/2 as the communication protocol for gRPC. Finally, we'll dive into the implementation architecture of gRPC and the language support stack built around it. Although the low-level details that we are going to discuss here may not be of much use in most gRPC applications, having a good understanding of the low-level communication details is quite helpful if you are designing a complex gRPC application or trying to debug existing applications.

RPC Flow

In an RPC system, the server implements a set of functions that can be invoked remotely. The client application can generate a stub that provides abstractions for the same functions offered from the server so that the client application can directly call stub functions that invoke the remote functions of the server application.

Let's look at the ProductInfo service that we discussed in Chapter 2 to understand how a remote procedure call works over the network. One of the functions that we implemented as part of our ProductInfo service is getProduct, where the client can retrieve product details by providing the product ID. Figure 4-1 illustrates the actions involved when the client calls a remote function.

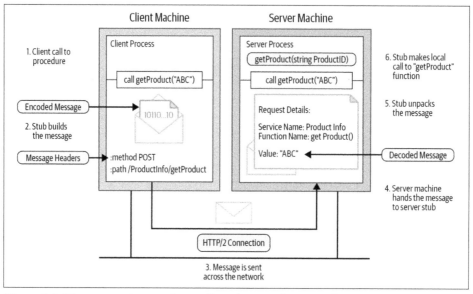

Figure 4-1. How a remote procedure call works over the network

As shown in Figure 4-1, we can identify the following key steps when the client calls the getProduct function in the generated stub:

❶ The client process calls the getProduct function in the generated stub.

❷ The client stub creates an HTTP POST request with the encoded message. In gRPC, all requests are HTTP POST requests with content-type prefixed with application/grpc. The remote function (/ProductInfo/getProduct) that it invokes is sent as a separate HTTP header.

❸ The HTTP request message is sent across the network to the server machine.

❹ When the message is received at the server, the server examines the message headers to see which service function needs to be called and hands over the message to the service stub.

❺ The service stub parses the message bytes into language-specific data structures.

❻ Then, using the parsed message, the service makes a local call to the getProduct function.

❼ The response from the service function is encoded and sent back to the client. The response message follows the same procedure that we observed on the client side (response→encode→HTTP response on the wire); the message is unpacked and its value returned to the waiting client process.

These steps are quite similar to most RPC systems like CORBA, Java RMI, etc. The main difference between gRPC here is the way that it encodes the message, which we saw in Figure 4-1. For encoding messages, gRPC uses protocol buffers. Protocol buffers (*https://oreil.ly/u9YJI*) are a language-agnostic, platform-neutral, extensible mechanism for serializing structured data. You define how you want your data to be structured once, then you can use the specially generated source code to easily write and read your structured data to and from a variety of data streams.

Let's dive into how gRPC uses protocol buffers to encode messages.

Message Encoding Using Protocol Buffers

As we discussed in previous chapters, gRPC uses protocol buffers to write the service definition for gRPC services. Defining the service using protocol buffers includes defining remote methods in the service and defining messages we want to send across the network. For example, let's take the getProduct method in the ProductInfo service. The getProduct method accepts a ProductID message as an input parameter and returns a Product message. We can define those input and output message structures using protocol buffers as shown in Example 4-1.

Example 4-1. Service definition of ProductInfo service with getProduct function

```
syntax = "proto3";

package ecommerce;

service ProductInfo {
    rpc getProduct(ProductID) returns (Product);
}

message Product {
```

```
    string id = 1;
    string name = 2;
    string description = 3;
    float price = 4;
}

message ProductID {
    string value = 1;
}
```

As per Example 4-1, the `ProductID` message carries a unique product ID. So it has only one field with a string type. The `Product` message has the structure required to represent the product. It is important to have a message defined correctly, because how you define the message determines how the messages get encoded. We will discuss how message definitions are used when encoding messages later in this section.

Now that we have the message definition, let's look at how to encode the message and generate the equivalent byte content. Normally this is handled by the generated source code for the message definition. All the supported languages have their own compilers to generate source code. As an application developer, you need to pass the message definition and generate source code to read and write the message.

Let's say we need to get product details for product ID 15; we create a message object with value equal to 15 and pass it to the `getProduct` function. The following code snippet shows how to create a `ProductID` message with value equal to 15 and pass it to the `getProduct` function to retrieve product details:

```
    product, err := c.GetProduct(ctx, &pb.ProductID{Value: "15"})
```

This code snippet is written in Go. Here, the `ProductID` message definition is in the generated source code. We create an instance of `ProductID` and set the value as 15. Similarly in the Java language, we use generated methods to create a `ProductID` instance as shown in the following code snippet:

```
    ProductInfoOuterClass.Product product = stub.getProduct(
            ProductInfoOuterClass.ProductID.newBuilder()
                    .setValue("15").build());
```

In the `ProductID` message structure that follows, there is one field called `value` with the field index 1. When we create a message instance with `value` equal to 15, the equivalent byte content consists of a field identifier for the `value` field followed by its encoded value. This field identifier is also known as a *tag*:

```
    message ProductID {
        string value = 1;
    }
```

This byte content structure looks like Figure 4-2, where each message field consists of a field identifier followed by its encoded value.

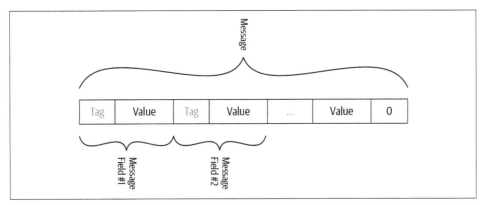

Figure 4-2. Protocol buffer encoded byte stream

This tag builds up two values: the field index and the wire type. The field index is the unique number we assigned to each message field when defining the message in the proto file. The wire type is based on the field type, which is the type of data that can enter the field. This wire type provides information to find the length of the value. Table 4-1 shows how wire types are mapped to field types. This is the predefined mapping of wire types and field types. You can refer to the official protocol buffers encoding document (*https://oreil.ly/xeLBr*) to get more insight into the mapping.

Table 4-1. Available wire types and corresponding field types

Wire type	Category	Field types
0	Varint	int32, int64, uint32, uint64, sint32, sint64, bool, enum
1	64-bit	fixed64, sfixed64, double
2	Length-delimited	string, bytes, embedded messages, packed repeated fields
3	Start group	groups (deprecated)
4	End group	groups (deprecated)
5	32-bit	fixed32, sfixed32, float

Once we know the field index and wire type of a certain field, we can determine the tag value of the field using the following equation. Here we left shift the binary representation of the field index by three digits and perform a bitwise union with the binary representation of the wire type value:

```
Tag value = (field_index << 3) | wire_type
```

Figure 4-3 shows how field index and wire type are arranged in a tag value.

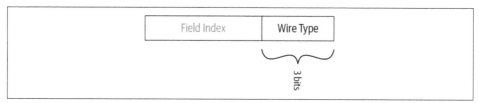

Field Index	Wire Type

3 bits

Figure 4-3. Structure of the tag value

Let's try to understand this terminology using the example that we used earlier. The ProductID message has one string field with field index equal to 1 and the wire type of string is 2. When we convert them to binary representation, the field index looks like 00000001 and the wire type looks like 00000010. When we put those values into the preceding equation, the tag value 10 is derived as follows:

```
Tag value = (00000001 << 3) | 00000010
          = 000 1010
```

The next step is to encode the value of the message field. Different encoding techniques are used by protocol buffers to encode the different types of data. For example, if it is a string value, the protocol buffer uses UTF-8 to encode the value and if it is an integer value with the int32 field type, it uses an encoding technique called varints. We will discuss different encoding techniques and when those techniques are applied in the next section in detail. For now, we will discuss how to encode a string value to complete the example.

In protocol buffers encoding, string values are encoded using UTF-8 encoding technique. UTF (Unicode Transformation Format) uses 8-bit blocks to represent a character. It is a variable-length character encoding technique that is also a preferred encoding technique in web pages and emails.

In our example, the value of the value field in the ProductID message is 15 and the UTF-8 encoded value of 15 is \x31 \x35. In UTF-8 encoding, the encoded value length is not fixed. In other words, the number of 8-bit blocks required to represent the encoded value is not fixed. It varies based upon the value of the message field. In our example, it is two blocks. So we need to pass the encoded value length (number of blocks the encoded value spans) before the encoded value. The hexadecimal representation of the encoded value of 15 will look like this:

```
A 02 31 35
```

The two righthand bytes here are the UTF-8 encoded value of 15. Value 0x02 represents the length of the encoded string value in 8-bit blocks.

When a message is encoded, its tags and values are concatenated into a byte stream. Figure 4-2 illustrates how field values are arranged into a byte stream when a message has multiple fields. The end of the stream is marked by sending a tag valued 0.

We have now completed encoding a simple message with a string field using protocol buffers. The protocol buffers support various field types and some field types have different encoding mechanisms. Let's quickly go through the encoding techniques used by protocol buffers.

Encoding Techniques

There are many encoding techniques supported by protocol buffers. Different encoding techniques are applied based on the type of data. For example, string values are encoded using UTF-8 character encoding, whereas int32 values are encoded using a technique called varints. Having knowledge about how data is encoded in each data type is important when designing the message definition because it allows us to set the most appropriate data type for each message field so that the messages are efficiently encoded at runtime.

In protocol buffers, supported field types are categorized into different groups and each group uses a different technique to encode the value. Listed in the next section are a few commonly used encoding techniques in protocol buffers.

Varints

Varints (variable length integers) are a method of serializing integers using one or more bytes. They're based on the idea that most numbers are not uniformly distributed. So the number of bytes allocated for each value is not fixed. It depends on the value. As per Table 4-1, field types like int32, int64, uint32, uint64, sint32, sint64, bool, and enum are grouped into varints and encoded as varints. Table 4-2 shows what field types are categorized under varints, and what each type is used for.

Table 4-2. Field type definitions

Field type	Definition
int32	A value type that represents signed integers with values that range from negative 2,147,483,648 to positive 2,147,483,647. Note this type is inefficient for encoding negative numbers.
int64	A value type that represents signed integers with values that range from negative 9,223,372,036,854,775,808 to positive 9,223,372,036,854,775,807. Note this type is inefficient for encoding negative numbers.
uint32	A value type that represents unsigned integers with values that range from 0 to 4,294,967,295.
uint64	A value type that represents unsigned integers with values that range from 0 to 18,446,744,073,709,551,615.
sint32	A value type that represents signed integers with values that range from negative 2,147,483,648 to positive 2,147,483,647. This more efficiently encodes negative numbers than regular int32s.
sint64	A value type that represents signed integers with values that range from negative 9,223,372,036,854,775,808 to positive 9,223,372,036,854,775,807. This more efficiently encodes negative numbers than regular int64s.
bool	A value type that represents two possible values, normally denoted as true or false.
enum	A value type that represents a set of named values.

In varints, each byte except the last byte has the most significant bit (MSB) set to indicate that there are further bytes to come. The lower 7 bits of each byte are used to store the two's complement representation of the number. Also, the least significant group comes first, which means that we should add a continuation bit to the low-order group.

Signed integers

Signed integers are types that represent both positive and negative integer values. Field types like sint32 and sint64 are considered signed integers. For signed types, zig-zag encoding is used to convert signed integers to unsigned ones. Then unsigned integers are encoded using varints encoding as mentioned previously.

In zigzag encoding, signed integers are mapped to unsigned integers in a zigzag way through negative and positive integers. Table 4-3 shows how mapping works in zigzag encoding.

Table 4-3. The zigzag encoding used in signed integers

Original value	Mapped value
0	0
-1	1
1	2
-2	3
2	4

As shown in Table 4-3, value zero is mapped to the original value of zero and other values are mapped to positive numbers in a zigzag way. The negative original values are mapped to odd positive numbers and positive original values are mapped to even positive numbers. After zigzag encoding, we get a positive number irrespective of the sign of the original value. Once we have a positive number, we perform varints to encode the value.

For negative integer values, it is recommended to use signed integer types like sint32 and sint64 because if we use a regular type such as int32 or int64, negative values are converted to binary using varints encoding. Varints encoding for a negative integer value needs more bytes to represent an equivalent binary value than a positive integer value. So the efficient way of encoding negative value is to convert the negative value to a positive number and then encode the positive value. In signed integer types like sint32, the negative values are first converted to positive values using zigzag encoding and then encoded using varints.

Nonvarint numbers

Nonvarint types are just the opposite of the varint type. They allocate a fixed number of bytes irrespective of the actual value. Protocol buffers use two wire types that categorize as nonvarint numbers. One is for the 64-bit data types like fixed64, sfixed64, and double. The other is for 32-bit data types like fixed32, sfixed32, and float.

String type

In protocol buffers, the string type belongs to the length-delimited wire type, which means that the value is a varint-encoded length followed by the specified number of bytes of data. String values are encoded using UTF-8 character encoding.

We just summarized the techniques used to encode commonly used data types. You can find a detailed explanation about protocol buffer encoding on the official page (*https://oreil.ly/hH_gL*).

Now that we have encoded the message using protocol buffers, the next step is to frame the message before sending it to the server over the network.

Length-Prefixed Message Framing

In common terms, the message-framing approach constructs information and communication so that the intended audience can easily extract the information. The same thing applies to gRPC communication as well. Once we have the encoded data to send to the other party, we need to package the data in a way that other parties can easily extract the information. In order to package the message to send over the network, gRPC uses a message-framing technique called length-prefix framing.

Length-prefix is a message-framing approach that writes the size of each message before writing the message itself. As you can see in Figure 4-4, before the encoded binary message there are 4 bytes allocated to specify the size of the message. In gRPC communication, 4 additional bytes are allocated for each message to set its size. The size of the message is a finite number, and allocating 4 bytes to represent the message size means gRPC communication can handle all messages up to 4 GB in size.

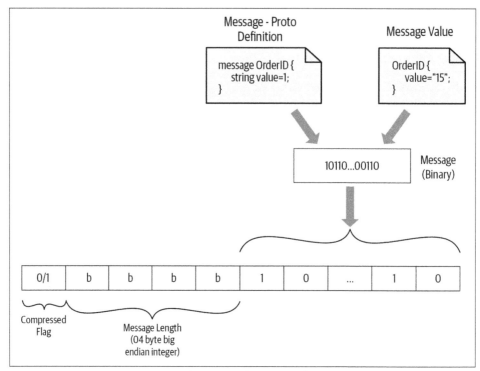

Figure 4-4. How a gRPC message frame uses length-prefix framing

As illustrated in Figure 4-4, when the message is encoded using protocol buffers, we get the message in binary format. Then we calculate the size of the binary content and add it before the binary content in big-endian format.

> Big-endian is a way of ordering binary data in the system or message. In big-endian format, the most significant value (the largest powers of two) in the sequence is stored at the lowest storage address.

In addition to the message size, the frame also has a 1-byte unsigned integer to indicate whether the data is compressed or not. A Compressed-Flag value of 1 indicates that the binary data is compressed using the mechanism declared in the Message-Encoding header, which is one of the headers declared in HTTP transport. The value 0 indicates that no encoding of message bytes has occurred. We will discuss HTTP headers supported in gRPC communication in detail in the next section.

So now the message is framed and it's ready to be sent over the network to the recipient. For a client request message, the recipient is the server. For a response message, the recipient is the client. On the recipient side, once a message is received, it first needs to read the first byte to check whether the message is compressed or not. Then the recipient reads the next four bytes to get the size of the encoded binary message. Once the size is known, the exact length of bytes can be read from the stream. For unary/simple messages, we will have only one length-prefixed message, and for streaming messages, we will have multiple length-prefixed messages to process.

Now you have a good understanding of how messages are prepared to deliver to the recipient over the network. In the next section, we are going to discuss how gRPC sends those length-prefixed messages over the network. Currently, the gRPC core supports three transport implementations: HTTP/2, Cronet (*https://oreil.ly/D0laq*), and in-process (*https://oreil.ly/lRgXF*). Among them, the most common transport for sending messages is HTTP/2. Let's discuss how gRPC utilizes the HTTP/2 network to send messages efficiently.

gRPC over HTTP/2

HTTP/2 is the second major version of the internet protocol HTTP. It was introduced to overcome some of the issues encountered with security, speed, etc. in the previous version (HTTP/1.1). HTTP/2 supports all of the core features of HTTP/1.1 but in a more efficient way. So applications written in HTTP/2 are faster, simpler, and more robust.

gRPC uses HTTP/2 as its transport protocol to send messages over the network. This is one of the reasons why gRPC is a high-performance RPC framework. Let's explore the relationship between gRPC and HTTP/2.

In HTTP/2, all communication between a client and server is performed over a single TCP connection that can carry any number of bidirectional flows of bytes. To understand the HTTP/2 process, you should be familiar with the following important terminology:

- *Stream:* A bidirectional flow of bytes within an established connection. A stream may carry one or more messages.

- *Frame:* The smallest unit of communication in HTTP/2. Each frame contains a frame header, which at a minimum identifies the stream to which the frame belongs.

- *Message:* A complete sequence of frames that map to a logical HTTP message that consists of one or more frames. This allows the messages to be multiplexed, by allowing the client and server to break down the message into independent frames, interleave them, and then reassemble them on the other side.

As you can see in Figure 4-5, the gRPC channel represents a connection to an endpoint, which is an HTTP/2 connection. When the client application creates a gRPC channel, behind the scenes it creates an HTTP/2 connection with the server. Once the channel is created we can reuse it to send multiple remote calls to the server. These remote calls are mapped to streams in HTTP/2. Messages that are sent in the remote call are sent as HTTP/2 frames. A frame may carry one gRPC length-prefixed message, or if a gRPC message is quite large it might span multiple data frames.

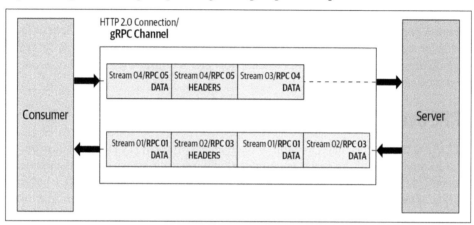

Figure 4-5. How gRPC semantics relate to HTTP/2

In the previous section, we discussed how to frame our message to a length-prefixed message. When we send them over the network as a request or response message, we need to send additional headers along with the message. Let's discuss how to structure request/response messages and which headers need to pass for each message in the next sections.

Request Message

The request message is the one that initiates the remote call. In gRPC, the request message is always triggered by the client application and it consists of three main components: request headers, the length-prefixed message, and the end of stream flag as shown in Figure 4-6. The remote call is initiated once the client sends request headers. Then, length-prefixed messages are sent in the call. Finally, the EOS (end of stream) flag is sent to notify the recipient that we finished sending the request message.

Figure 4-6. Sequence of message elements in request message

Let's use the same `getProduct` function in the `ProductInfo` service to explain how the request message is sent in HTTP/2 frames. When we call the `getProduct` function, the client initiates a call by sending request headers as shown here:

```
HEADERS (flags = END_HEADERS)
:method = POST ❶
:scheme = http ❷
:path = /ProductInfo/getProduct ❸
:authority = abc.com ❹
te = trailers ❺
grpc-timeout = 1S ❻
content-type = application/grpc ❼
grpc-encoding = gzip ❽
authorization = Bearer xxxxxx ❾
```

❶ Defines the HTTP method. For gRPC, the `:method` header is always `POST`.

❷ Defines the HTTP scheme. If TLS (Transport Level Security) is enabled, the scheme is set to "https," otherwise it is "http."

❸ Defines the endpoint path. For gRPC, this value is constructed as "/" {service name} "/" {method name}.

❹ Defines the virtual hostname of the target URI.

❺ Defines detection of incompatible proxies. For gRPC, the value must be "trailers."

❻ Defines call timeout. If not specified, the server should assume an infinite timeout.

❼ Defines the content-type. For gRPC, the content-type should begin with `applica tion/grpc`. If not, gRPC servers will respond with an HTTP status of 415 (Unsupported Media Type).

❽ Defines the message compression type. Possible values are `identity`, `gzip`, `deflate`, `snappy`, and {custom}.

❾ This is optional metadata. `authorization` metadata is used to access the secure endpoint.

Some other notes on this example:

- Header names starting with ":" are called reserved headers and HTTP/2 requires reserved headers to appear before other headers.

- Headers passed in gRPC communication are categorized into two types: call-definition headers and custom metadata.

- Call-definition headers are predefined headers supported by HTTP/2. Those headers should be sent before custom metadata.

- Custom metadata is an arbitrary set of key-value pairs defined by the application layer. When you are defining custom metadata, you need to make sure not to use a header name starting with grpc-. This is listed as a reserved name in the gRPC core.

Once the client initiates the call with the server, the client sends length-prefixed messages as HTTP/2 data frames. If the length-prefixed message doesn't fit one data frame, it can span to multiple data frames. The end of the request message is indicated by adding an END_STREAM flag on the last DATA frame. When no data remains to be sent but we need to close the request stream, the implementation must send an empty data frame with the END_STREAM flag:

```
DATA (flags = END_STREAM)
<Length-Prefixed Message>
```

This is just an overview of the structure of the gRPC request message. You can find more details in the official gRPC GitHub repository (*https://oreil.ly/VIhYs*).

Similar to the request message, the response message also has its own structure. Let's look at the structure of response messages and the related headers.

Response Message

The response message is generated by the server in response to the client's request. Similar to the request message, in most cases the response message also consists of three main components: response headers, length-prefixed messages, and trailers. When there is no length-prefixed message to send as a response to the client, the response message consists only of headers and trailers as shown in Figure 4-7.

Figure 4-7. Sequence of message elements in a response message

Let's look at the same example to explain the HTTP/2 framing sequence of the response message. When the server sends a response to the client, it first sends response headers as shown here:

```
HEADERS (flags = END_HEADERS)
:status = 200 ❶
grpc-encoding = gzip ❷
content-type = application/grpc ❸
```

❶ Indicates the status of the HTTP request.

❷ Defines the message compression type. Possible values include identity, gzip, deflate, snappy, and {custom}.

❸ Defines the content-type. For gRPC, the content-type should begin with appli cation/grpc.

 Similar to the request headers, custom metadata that contains an arbitrary set of key-value pairs defined by the application layer can be set in the response headers.

Once the server sends response headers, length-prefixed messages are sent as HTTP/2 data frames in the call. Similar to the request message, if the length-prefixed message doesn't fit one data frame, it can span to multiple data frames. As shown in the following, the END_STREAM flag isn't sent with data frames. It is sent as a separate header called a trailer:

```
DATA
<Length-Prefixed Message>
```

In the end, trailers are sent to notify the client that we finished sending the response message. Trailers also carry the status code and status message of the request:

```
HEADERS (flags = END_STREAM, END_HEADERS)
grpc-status = 0 # OK ❶
grpc-message = xxxxxx ❷
```

❶ Defines the gRPC status code. gRPC uses a set of well-defined status codes. You can find the definition of status codes in the official gRPC documentation (*https://oreil.ly/3MH72*).

❷ Defines the description of the error. This is optional. This is only set when there is an error in processing the request.

Trailers are also delivered as HTTP/2 header frames but at the end of the response message. The end of the response stream is indicated by setting the END_STREAM flag in trailer headers. Additionally, it contains the grpc-status and grpc-message headers.

In certain scenarios, there can be an immediate failure in the request call. In those cases, the server needs to send a response back without the data frames. So the server sends only trailers as a response. Those trailers are also delivered as an HTTP/2 header frame and also contain the END_STREAM flag. Additionally, the following headers are included in trailers:

- HTTP-Status → :status
- Content-Type → content-type
- Status → grpc-status
- Status-Message → grpc-message

Now that we know how a gRPC message flows over an HTTP/2 connection, let's try to understand the message flow of different communication patterns in gRPC.

Understanding the Message Flow in gRPC Communication Patterns

In the previous chapter, we discussed four communication patterns supported by gRPC. They are simple RPC, server-streaming RPC, client-streaming RPC, and bidirectional-streaming RPC. We also discussed how those communication patterns work using real-world use cases. In this section, we are going to look at those patterns again from a different angle. Let's discuss how each pattern works at the transport level with the knowledge we collected in this chapter.

Simple RPC

In simple RPC you always have a single request and a single response in the communication between the gRPC server and gRPC client. As shown in Figure 4-8, the request message contains headers followed by a length-prefixed message, which can span one or more data frames. An end of stream (EOS) flag is added at the end of the message to half-close the connection at the client side and mark the end of the request message. Here "half-close the connection" means the client closes the connection on its side so the client is no longer able to send messages to the server but still can listen to the incoming messages from the server. The server creates the response message only after receiving the complete message on the server side. The response message contains a header frame followed by a length-prefixed message. Communication ends once the server sends the trailing header with status details.

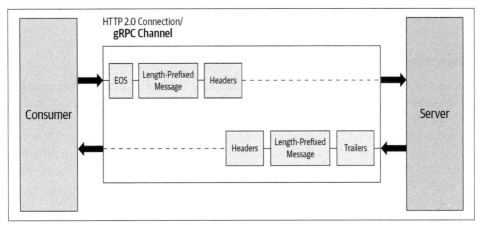

Figure 4-8. Simple RPC: message flow

This is the simplest communication pattern. Let's move on to a bit more complex server-streaming RPC scenario.

Server-streaming RPC

From the client perspective, both simple RPC and server-streaming RPC have the same request message flow. In both cases, we send one request message. The main difference is on the server side. Rather than sending one response message to the client, the server sends multiple messages. The server waits until it receives the completed request message and sends the response headers and multiple length-prefixed messages as shown in Figure 4-9. Communication ends once the server sends the trailing header with status details.

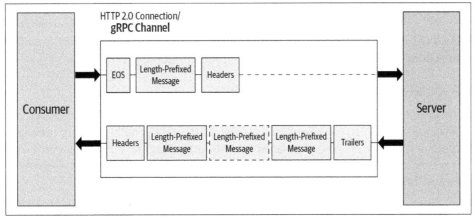

Figure 4-9. Server-streaming RPC: message flow

Now let's look at client-streaming RPC, which is pretty much the opposite of server-streaming RPC.

Client-streaming RPC

In client-streaming RPC, the client sends multiple messages to the server and the server sends one response message in reply. The client first sets up the connection with the server by sending the header frames. Once the connection is set up, the client sends multiple length-prefixed messages as data frames to the server as shown in Figure 4-10. In the end, the client half-closes the connection by sending an EOS flag in the last data frame. In the meantime, the server reads the messages received from the client. Once it receives all messages, the server sends a response message along with the trailing header and closes the connection.

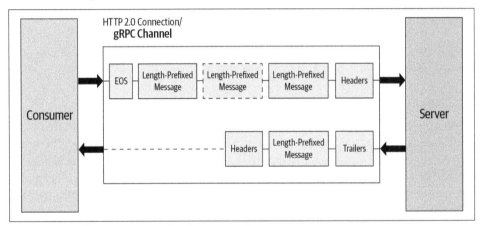

Figure 4-10. Client-streaming RPC: message flow

Now let's move onto the last communication pattern, bidirectional RPC, in which the client and server are both sending multiple messages to each other until they close the connection.

Bidirectional-streaming RPC

In this pattern, the client sets up the connection by sending header frames. Once the connection is set up, the client and server both send length-prefixed messages without waiting for the other to finish. As shown in Figure 4-11, both client and server send messages simultaneously. Both can end the connection at their side, meaning they can't send any more messages.

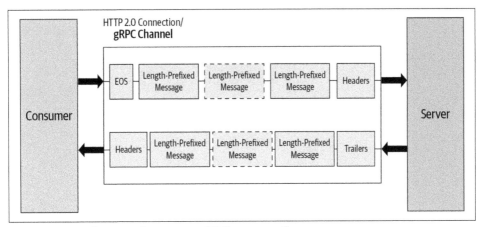

Figure 4-11. Bidirectional-streaming RPC: message flow

With that, we have come to the end of our in-depth tour of gRPC communication. Network and transport-related operations in communication are normally handled at the gRPC core layer and you don't need to be aware of the details as a gRPC application developer.

Before wrapping up this chapter, let's look at the gRPC implementation architecture and the language stack.

gRPC Implementation Architecture

As shown in Figure 4-12, gRPC implementation can be divided into multiple layers. The base layer is the gRPC core layer. It is a thin layer and it abstracts all the network operations from the upper layers so that application developers can easily make RPC calls over the network. The core layer also provides extensions to the core functionality. Some of the extension points are authentication filters to handle call security and a deadline filter to implement call deadlines, etc.

gRPC is natively supported by the C/C++, Go, and Java languages. gRPC also provides language bindings in many popular languages such as Python, Ruby, PHP, etc. These language bindings are wrappers over the low-level C API.

Finally, the application code goes on top of language bindings. This application layer handles the application logic and data encoding logic. Normally developers generate source code for data encoding logic using compilers provided by different languages. For example, if we use protocol buffers for encoding data, the protocol buffer compiler can be used to generate source code. So developers can write their application logic by invoking the methods of generated source code.

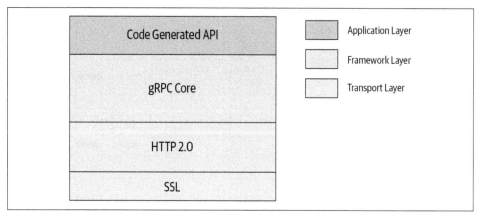

Figure 4-12. gRPC native implementation architecture

With that, we have covered most of the low-level implementation and execution details of gRPC-based applications. As an application developer, it is always better to have an understanding of the low-level details about the techniques you're going to use in the application. It not only helps to design robust applications, but also helps in troubleshooting application issues easily.

Summary

gRPC builds on top of two fast and efficient protocols called protocol buffers and HTTP/2. Protocol buffers are a data serialization protocol that is a language-agnostic, platform-neutral, and extensible mechanism for serializing structured data. Once serialized, this protocol produces a binary payload that is smaller in size than a normal JSON payload and is strongly typed. This serialized binary payload then travels over the binary transport protocol called HTTP/2.

HTTP/2 is the next major version of the internet protocol HTTP. HTTP/2 is fully multiplexed, which means that HTTP/2 can send multiple requests for data in parallel over a single TCP connection. This makes applications written in HTTP/2 faster, simpler, and more robust than others.

All these factors make gRPC a high-performance RPC framework.

In this chapter we covered low-level details about gRPC communication. These details may be not essential to develop a gRPC application, because they are already handled by the library, but understanding low-level gRPC message flow is absolutely essential when it comes to troubleshooting gRPC communication-related issues when you use gRPC in production. In the next chapter, we'll discuss some advanced capabilities provided by gRPC to cater to real-world requirements.

gRPC: Beyond the Basics

When you build real-world gRPC applications you may have to augment them with various capabilities to meet requirements such as intercepting incoming and outgoing RPC, handling network delays resiliently, handling errors, sharing metadata between services and consumers, and so on.

 To maintain consistency, all samples in this chapter are explained using Go. If you're more familiar with Java, you can refer to the Java samples in the source code repository for the same use cases.

In this chapter, you will learn some key advanced gRPC capabilities including using gRPC interceptors to intercept RPCs on the server and client sides, using deadlines to specify the wait time for an RPC to complete, error-handling best practices on the server and client sides, using multiplexing to run multiple services on the same server, sharing custom metadata between applications, using load-balancing and name resolution techniques when calling other services, and compressing RPC calls to effectively use the network bandwidth.

Let's begin our discussion with gRPC interceptors.

Interceptors

As you build gRPC applications, you may want to execute some common logic before or after the execution of the remote function, for either client or server applications. In gRPC you can intercept that RPC's execution to meet certain requirements such as logging, authentication, metrics, etc., using an extension mechanism called an *interceptor*. gRPC provides simple APIs to implement and install interceptors in your client and server gRPC applications. They are one of the key extension mechanisms in gRPC and are quite useful in use cases such as logging, authentication, authorization, metrics, tracing, and any other customer requirements.

> Interceptors are not supported in all languages that support gRPC, and the implementation of interceptors in each language may be different. In this book we only cover Go and Java.

gRPC interceptors can be categorized into two types based on the type of RPC calls they intercept. For unary RPC you can use *unary interceptors*, while for streaming RPC you can use *streaming interceptors*. These interceptors can be used on the gRPC server side or on the gRPC client side. First, let's start by looking at using interceptors on the server side.

Server-Side Interceptors

When a client invokes a remote method of a gRPC service, you can execute a common logic prior to the execution of the remote methods by using a server-side interceptor. This helps when you need to apply certain features such as authentication prior to invoking the remote method. As shown in Figure 5-1, you can plug one or more interceptors into any gRPC server that you develop. For example, to plug a new server-side interceptor into your OrderManagement gRPC service, you can implement the interceptor and register it when you create the gRPC server.

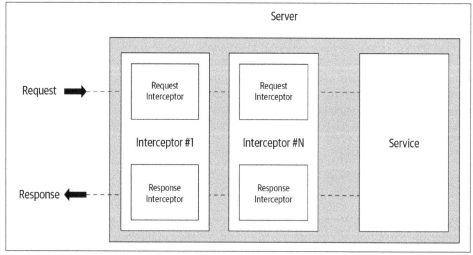

Figure 5-1. Server-side interceptors

On the server side, the unary interceptor allows you to intercept the unary RPC call while the streaming interceptor intercepts the streaming RPC. Let's first discuss server-side unary interceptors.

Unary interceptor

If you want to intercept the unary RPC of your gRPC service at the server side, you'll need to implement a unary interceptor for your gRPC server. As shown in the Go code snippet in Example 5-1, you can do this by implementing a function of type `UnaryServerInterceptor` and registering that function when you create a gRPC server. `UnaryServerInterceptor` is the type for a server-side unary interceptor with the following signature:

```
func(ctx context.Context, req interface{}, info *UnaryServerInfo,
                        handler UnaryHandler) (resp interface{}, err error)
```

Inside this function you get full control of all unary RPC calls that are coming to your gRPC server.

Example 5-1. gRPC server-side unary interceptor

```
// Server - Unary Interceptor
func orderUnaryServerInterceptor(ctx context.Context, req interface{},
                        info *grpc.UnaryServerInfo, handler grpc.UnaryHandler)
                        (interface{}, error) {

        // Preprocessing logic
        // Gets info about the current RPC call by examining the args passed in
        log.Println("======= [Server Interceptor] ", info.FullMethod) ❶


        // Invoking the handler to complete the normal execution of a unary RPC.
        m, err := handler(ctx, req) ❷

        // Post processing logic
        log.Printf(" Post Proc Message : %s", m) ❸
        return m, err ❹
}


// ...

func main() {

    ...
        // Registering the Interceptor at the server-side.
        s := grpc.NewServer(
                grpc.UnaryInterceptor(orderUnaryServerInterceptor)) ❺
    ...
```

❶ Preprocessing phase: this is where you can intercept the message prior to invoking the respective RPC.

❷ Invoking the RPC method via `UnaryHandler`.

❸ Postprocessing phase: you can process the response from the RPC invocation.

❹ Sending back the RPC response.

❺ Registering the unary interceptor with the gRPC server.

The implementation of a server-side unary interceptor can usually be divided into three parts: preprocessing, invoking the RPC method, and postprocessing. As the name implies, the preprocessor phase is executed prior to invoking the remote method intended in the RPC call. In the preprocessor phase, users can get info about the current RPC call by examining the args passed in, such as RPC context, RPC request, and server information. Thus, during the preprocessor phase you can even modify the RPC call.

Then, in the invoker phase, you have to call the gRPC `UnaryHandler` to invoke the RPC method. Once you invoke the RPC, the postprocessor phase is executed. This means that the response for the RPC call goes through the postprocessor phase. In the phase, you can deal with the returned reply and error when required. Once the postprocessor phase is completed, you need to return the message and the error as the return parameters of your interceptor function. If no postprocessing is required, you can simply return the handler call (`handler(ctx, req)`).

Next, let's discuss streaming interceptors.

Stream interceptor

The server-side streaming interceptor intercepts any streaming RPC calls that the gRPC server deals with. The stream interceptor includes a preprocessing phase and a stream operation interception phase.

As shown in the Go code snippet in Example 5-2, suppose that we want to intercept streaming RPC calls of the `OrderManagement` service. `StreamServerInterceptor` is the type for server-side stream interceptors. `orderServerStreamInterceptor` is an interceptor function of type `StreamServerInterceptor` with the signature:

```
func(srv interface{}, ss ServerStream, info *StreamServerInfo,
                              handler StreamHandler) error
```

Similar to a unary interceptor, in the preprocessor phase, you can intercept a streaming RPC call before it goes to the service implementation. After the preprocessor phase, you can then invoke the `StreamHandler` to complete the execution of RPC invocation of the remote method. After the preprocessor phase, you can intercept the streaming RPC message by using an interface known as a wrapper stream that implements the `grpc.ServerStream` interface. You can pass this wrapper structure when you invoke `grpc.StreamHandler` with `handler(srv, newWrappedStream(ss))`. The wrapper of `grpc.ServerStream` intercepts the streaming messages sent or received by the gRPC service. It implements the `SendMsg` and `RecvMsg` functions, which will be invoked when the service receives or sends an RPC streaming message.

Example 5-2. gRPC server-side streaming interceptor

```
// Server - Streaming Interceptor
// wrappedStream wraps around the embedded grpc.ServerStream,
// and intercepts the RecvMsg and SendMsg method call.

type wrappedStream struct { ❶
        grpc.ServerStream
}

❷
func (w *wrappedStream) RecvMsg(m interface{}) error {
        log.Printf("====== [Server Stream Interceptor Wrapper] " +
                "Receive a message (Type: %T) at %s",
                m, time.Now().Format(time.RFC3339))
        return w.ServerStream.RecvMsg(m)
}

❸
func (w *wrappedStream) SendMsg(m interface{}) error {
        log.Printf("====== [Server Stream Interceptor Wrapper] " +
                "Send a message (Type: %T) at %v",
                m, time.Now().Format(time.RFC3339))
        return w.ServerStream.SendMsg(m)
}

❹
func newWrappedStream(s grpc.ServerStream) grpc.ServerStream {
        return &wrappedStream{s}
}

❺
func orderServerStreamInterceptor(srv interface{},
        ss grpc.ServerStream, info *grpc.StreamServerInfo,
        handler grpc.StreamHandler) error {
        log.Println("====== [Server Stream Interceptor] ",
                info.FullMethod) ❻
        err := handler(srv, newWrappedStream(ss)) ❼
        if err != nil {
                log.Printf("RPC failed with error %v", err)
        }
        return err
```

```
}

...
// Registering the interceptor
s := grpc.NewServer(
              grpc.StreamInterceptor(orderServerStreamInterceptor)) ❽

...
```

❶ Wrapper stream of the grpc.ServerStream.

❷ Implementing the RecvMsg function of the wrapper to process messages received
    with stream RPC.

❸ Implementing the SendMsg function of the wrapper to process messages sent with
    stream RPC.

❹ Creating an instance of the new wrapper stream.

❺ Streaming interceptor implementation.

❻ Preprocessor phase.

❼ Invoking the streaming RPC with the wrapper stream.

❽ Registering the interceptor.

To understand the behavior of the streaming interceptor on the server side, look at
the following output from the gRPC server logs. Based on the order in which each log
message is printed you can identify the behavior of the streaming interceptor. The
streaming remote method that we have invoked here is SearchOrders, which is a
server-streaming RPC:

```
[Server Stream Interceptor]  /ecommerce.OrderManagement/searchOrders
[Server Stream Interceptor Wrapper] Receive a message

Matching Order Found : 102 -> Writing Order to the stream ...
[Server Stream Interceptor Wrapper] Send a message...
Matching Order Found : 104 -> Writing Order to the stream ...
[Server Stream Interceptor Wrapper] Send a message...
```

Client-side interceptor terminology is quite similar to that of server-side interceptors,
with some subtle variations as to the interfaces and function signatures. Let's move on
to the details of client-side interceptors.

Client-Side Interceptors

When a client invokes an RPC call to invoke a remote method of a gRPC service, you can intercept those RPC calls on the client side. As shown in Figure 5-2, with client-side interceptors, you can intercept unary RPC calls as well as streaming RPC calls.

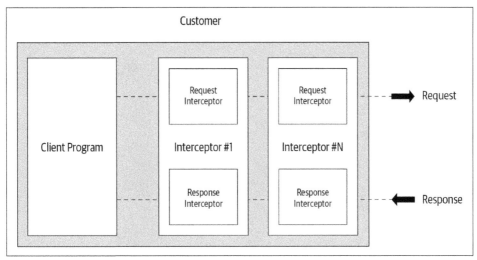

Figure 5-2. Client-side interceptors

This is particularly useful when you need to implement certain reusable features, such as securely calling a gRPC service outside the client application code.

Unary interceptor

A client-side unary RPC interceptor is used for intercepting the unary RPC client side. `UnaryClientInterceptor` is the type for a client-side unary interceptor that has a function signature as follows:

```
func(ctx context.Context, method string, req, reply interface{},
        cc *ClientConn, invoker UnaryInvoker, opts ...CallOption) error
```

As we saw with the server-side unary interceptor, the client-side unary interceptor has different phases. Example 5-3 shows the basic Go implementation of a unary interceptor on the client side. In the preprocessor phase, you can intercept the RPC calls before invoking the remote method. Here you will have access to the information about the current RPC call by examining the args passed in, such as RPC context, method string, request to be sent, and `CallOptions` configured. So, you can even modify the original RPC call before it is sent to the server application. Then using the `UnaryInvoker` argument you can invoke the actual unary RPC. In the postprocessor phase, you can access the response or the error results of the RPC invocation.

Example 5-3. gRPC client-side unary interceptor

```
func orderUnaryClientInterceptor(
        ctx context.Context, method string, req, reply interface{},
        cc *grpc.ClientConn,
        invoker grpc.UnaryInvoker, opts ...grpc.CallOption) error {
        // Preprocessor phase
        log.Println("Method : " + method) ❶

        // Invoking the remote method
        err := invoker(ctx, method, req, reply, cc, opts...) ❷

        // Postprocessor phase
        log.Println(reply) ❸

        return err ❹
}
...

func main() {
        // Setting up a connection to the server.
        conn, err := grpc.Dial(address, grpc.WithInsecure(),
                grpc.WithUnaryInterceptor(orderUnaryClientInterceptor)) ❺
...
```

❶ Preprocessing phase has access to the RPC request prior to sending it out to the server.

❷ Invoking the RPC method via `UnaryInvoker`.

❸ Postprocessing phase where you can process the response or error results.

❹ Returning an error back to the gRPC client application along with a reply, which is passed as an argument.

❺ Setting up a connection to the server by passing a unary interceptor as a dial option.

Registering the interceptor function is done inside the `grpc.Dial` operation using `grpc.WithUnaryInterceptor`.

Stream interceptor

The client-side streaming interceptor intercepts any streaming RPC calls that the gRPC client deals with. The implementation of the client-side stream interceptor is quite similar to that of the server side. `StreamClientInterceptor` is the type for a client-side stream interceptor; it is a function type with this signature:

```
func(ctx context.Context, desc *StreamDesc, cc *ClientConn,
                          method string, streamer Streamer,
                          opts ...CallOption) (ClientStream, error)
```

As shown in Example 5-4, the client-side stream interceptor implementation includes preprocessing and stream operation interception.

Example 5-4. gRPC client-side stream interceptor

```
func clientStreamInterceptor(
        ctx context.Context, desc *grpc.StreamDesc,
        cc *grpc.ClientConn, method string,
        streamer grpc.Streamer, opts ...grpc.CallOption)
        (grpc.ClientStream, error) {
        log.Println("======= [Client Interceptor] ", method) ❶
        s, err := streamer(ctx, desc, cc, method, opts...) ❷
        if err != nil {
                return nil, err
        }
        return newWrappedStream(s), nil ❸
}


type wrappedStream struct { ❹
        grpc.ClientStream
}

func (w *wrappedStream) RecvMsg(m interface{}) error { ❺
        log.Printf("====== [Client Stream Interceptor] " +
                "Receive a message (Type: %T) at %v",
                m, time.Now().Format(time.RFC3339))
        return w.ClientStream.RecvMsg(m)
}

func (w *wrappedStream) SendMsg(m interface{}) error { ❻
        log.Printf("====== [Client Stream Interceptor] " +
                "Send a message (Type: %T) at %v",
                m, time.Now().Format(time.RFC3339))
        return w.ClientStream.SendMsg(m)
}

func newWrappedStream(s grpc.ClientStream) grpc.ClientStream {
        return &wrappedStream{s}
}

...

func main() {
        // Setting up a connection to the server.
        conn, err := grpc.Dial(address, grpc.WithInsecure(),
```

```
                grpc.WithStreamInterceptor(clientStreamInterceptor)) ❼
    . . .
```

❶ Preprocessing phase has access to the RPC request prior to sending it out to the server.

❷ Calling the passed-in streamer to get a `ClientStream`.

❸ Wrapping around the `ClientStream`, overloading its methods with intercepting logic, and returning it to the client application.

❹ Wrapper stream of `grpc.ClientStream`.

❺ Function to intercept messages received from streaming RPC.

❻ Function to intercept messages sent from streaming RPC.

❼ Registering a streaming interceptor.

Intercepting for stream operations is done via a wrapper implementation of the stream where you have to implement a new structure wrapping `grpc.ClientStream`. Here you implement two wrapped stream methods, `RecvMsg` and `SendMsg`, that can be used to intercept streaming messages received or sent from the client side. The registration of the interceptor is the same as for the unary interceptor and is done with the `grpc.Dial` operation.

Let's look at deadlines, another capability you'll often need to apply when calling gRPC services from the client application.

Deadlines

Deadlines and timeouts are two commonly used patterns in distributed computing. *Timeouts* allow you to specify how long a client application can wait for an RPC to complete before it terminates with an error. A timeout is usually specified as a duration and locally applied at each client side. For example, a single request may consist of multiple downstream RPCs that chain together multiple services. So we can apply timeouts, relative to each RPC, at each service invocation. Therefore, timeouts cannot be directly applied for the entire life cycle of the request. That's where we need to use deadlines.

A *deadline* is expressed in absolute time from the beginning of a request (even if the API presents them as a duration offset) and applied across multiple service invocations. The application that initiates the request sets the deadline and the entire request chain needs to respond by the deadline. gRPC APIs supports using deadlines for your RPC. For many reasons, it is always good practice to use deadlines in your gRPC applications. gRPC communication happens over the network, so there can be delays between the RPC calls and responses. Also, in certain cases the gRPC service itself can take more time to respond depending on the service's business logic. When client applications are developed without using deadlines, they infinitely wait for a response for RPC requests that are initiated and resources will be held for all in-flight requests. This puts the service as well as the client at risk of running out of resources, increasing the latency of the service; this could even crash the entire gRPC service.

The example scenario shown in Figure 5-3 illustrates a gRPC client application calling a product management service that again invokes the inventory service.

The client application sets a deadline offset (i.e., deadline = current time + offset) of 50 ms. The network latency between the client and ProductMgt service is 0 ms and the processing latency of the ProductMgt service is 20 ms. The product management service has to set a deadline offset of 30 ms. Since the inventory service takes 30 ms to respond, the deadline event would occur on both client sides (ProductMgt invokes the Inventory service and the client application).

The latency added from the business logic of the ProductMgt service is 20 ms. Then the ProductMgt service's invocation logic triggers the deadline-exceeded scenario and propagates it back to the client application as well. Therefore, when using deadlines, make sure that they are applied across all services.

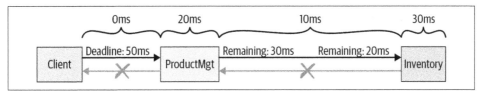

Figure 5-3. Using deadlines when calling services

A client application can set a deadline when it initiates a connection with a gRPC service. Once the RPC call is made, the client application waits for the duration specified by the deadline; if the response for the RPC call is not received within that time, the RPC call is terminated with a DEADLINE_EXCEEDED error.

Let's look at a real-world example of using deadlines when invoking gRPC services. In the same OrderManagement service use case, suppose the AddOrder RPC takes a significant amount of time to complete (we've simulated this with the introduction of a delay into the AddOrder method of the OrderManagement gRPC service). But the client application only waits until the response is no longer useful to it. For example, the duration that AddOrder takes to respond is two seconds, while the client only waits two seconds for a response. To implement this (as shown in the Go code snippet shown in Example 5-5), the client application can set the two-second timeout with the context.WithDeadline operation. We have used the status package to process error code; we'll discuss this in detail in the error-handling section.

Example 5-5. gRPC deadlines for the client application

```
conn, err := grpc.Dial(address, grpc.WithInsecure())
if err != nil {
    log.Fatalf("did not connect: %v", err)
}
defer conn.Close()
client := pb.NewOrderManagementClient(conn)

clientDeadline := time.Now().Add(
    time.Duration(2 * time.Second))
ctx, cancel := context.WithDeadline(
    context.Background(), clientDeadline) ❶

defer cancel()

// Add Order
order1 := pb.Order{Id: "101",
    Items:[]string{"iPhone XS", "Mac Book Pro"},
    Destination:"San Jose, CA",
    Price:2300.00}
res, addErr := client.AddOrder(ctx, &order1) ❷

if addErr != nil {
    got := status.Code(addErr) ❸
    log.Printf("Error Occured -> addOrder : , %v:", got) ❹
} else {
    log.Print("AddOrder Response -> ", res.Value)
}
```

❶ Setting a two-second deadline on the current context.

❷ Invoking the AddOrder remote method and capturing any possible errors into addErr.

❸ Using the status package to determine the error code.

❹ If the invocation exceeds the specified deadline, it should return an error of the type DEADLINE_EXCEEDED.

So how should we determine the ideal value for the deadline? There is no single answer to that question, but you need to consider several factors in making that choice; mainly, the end-to-end latency of each service that we invoke, which RPCs are serial and which RPCs can be made in parallel, the latency of the underlying network, and the deadline values of the downstream services. Once you are able to come up with the initial value for the deadline, fine-tune it based on the operating condition of the gRPC applications.

 Setting the gRPC deadline in Go is done through Go's context package (*https://oreil.ly/OTrmY*), where WithDeadline is a built-in function. In Go, context is often used to pass down common data that can be used by all downstream operations. Once this is called from the gRPC client application, the gRPC library at the client side creates a required gRPC header to represent the deadline between the client and server applications. In Java, this is slightly different, as the implementation directly comes from the io.grpc.stub.* package's stub implementation where you will set the gRPC deadline with blockingStub.withDeadlineAfter(long, java.util.concurrent.TimeUnit). Please refer to the code repository for details of the Java implementation.

When it comes to deadlines in gRPC, both the client and server can make their own independent and local determination about whether the RPC was successful; this means their conclusions may not match. For instance, in our example, when the client meets the DEADLINE_EXCEEDED condition, the service may still try to respond. So, the service application needs to determine whether the current RPC is still valid or not. From the server side, you can also detect when the client has reached the deadline specified when invoking the RPC. Inside the AddOrder operation, you can check for ctx.Err() == context.DeadlineExceeded to find out whether the client has already met the deadline exceeded state, and then abandon the RPC at the server side and return an error (this is often implemented using a nonblocking select construct in Go).

Similar to deadlines, there can be certain situations in which your client or server application wants to terminate the ongoing gRPC communication. This is where gRPC cancellation becomes useful.

Cancellation

In a gRPC connection between a client and server application, both the client and server make independent and local determinations of the success of the call. For instance, you could have an RPC that finishes successfully on the server side but fails on the client side. Similarly, there can be various conditions where the client and server may end up with different conclusions on the results of an RPC. When either the client or server application wants to terminate the RPC this can be done by *canceling* the RPC. Once the RPC is canceled, no further RPC-related messaging can be done and the fact that one party has canceled the RPC is propagated to the other side.

In Go, similar to deadlines, the cancellation capability is provided via the context package (*https://oreil.ly/OTrmY*) where WithCancel is a built-in function. Once this is called from the gRPC application, the gRPC library on the client side creates a required gRPC header to represent the gRPC termination between the client and server applications.

Let's take the example of bidirectional streaming between the client and server applications. In the Go code sample shown in Example 5-6, you can obtain the cancel function from the context.WithTimeout call. Once you have the reference to cancel, you can call it at any location where you intend to terminate the RPC.

Example 5-6. gRPC cancellation

```
ctx, cancel := context.WithTimeout(context.Background(), 10*time.Second) ❶


streamProcOrder, _ := client.ProcessOrders(ctx) ❷
_ = streamProcOrder.Send(&wrapper.StringValue{Value:"102"}) ❸
_ = streamProcOrder.Send(&wrapper.StringValue{Value:"103"})
_ = streamProcOrder.Send(&wrapper.StringValue{Value:"104"})

channel := make(chan bool, 1)

go asncClientBidirectionalRPC(streamProcOrder, channel)
time.Sleep(time.Millisecond * 1000)

// Canceling the RPC
cancel() ❹
log.Printf("RPC Status : %s", ctx.Err()) ❺

_ = streamProcOrder.Send(&wrapper.StringValue{Value:"101"})
_ = streamProcOrder.CloseSend()

<- channel

func asncClientBidirectionalRPC (
    streamProcOrder pb.OrderManagement_ProcessOrdersClient, c chan bool) {
...
                combinedShipment, errProcOrder := streamProcOrder.Recv()
                if errProcOrder != nil {
                        log.Printf("Error Receiving messages %v", errProcOrder) ❻
...
}
```

❶ Obtaining the reference to cancel.

❷ Invoking the streaming RPC.

❸   Sending messages to the service via the stream.

❹   Canceling RPC/terminating RPC from the client side.

❺   Status of the current context.

❻   Returning context canceled error when trying to receive messages from a canceled context.

When one party cancels the RPC, the other party can determine it by checking the context. In this example, the server application can check whether the current context is canceled by using `stream.Context().Err() == context.Canceled`.

As you have seen in the application of deadlines as well as cancellation, handling errors with RPC is a very common requirement. In the next section, we look at gRPC error-handling techniques in detail.

Error Handling

When we invoke a gRPC call, the client receives a response with a successful status or an error with the corresponding error status. The client application needs to be written in such a way that you handle all the potential errors and error conditions. The server application requires you to handle errors as well as generate the appropriate errors with corresponding status codes.

When an error occurs, gRPC returns one of its error-status codes with an optional error message that provides more details of the error condition. The status object is composed of an integer code and a string message that are common to all gRPC implementations for different languages.

gRPC uses a set of well-defined gRPC-specific status codes. This includes status codes such as the following:

OK
> Successful status; not an error.

CANCELLED
> The operation was canceled, typically by the caller.

DEADLINE_EXCEEDED
> The deadline expired before the operation could complete.

INVALID_ARGUMENT
> The client specified an invalid argument.

Table 5-1 shows the available gRPC error codes and the description of each error code. The complete list of error codes can be found in the gRPC official documentation (*https://oreil.ly/LiNLn*), or in the documentation for Go (*https://oreil.ly/E61Q0*) and Java (*https://oreil.ly/Ugtg0*).

Table 5-1. gRPC error codes

Code	Number	Description
OK	0	Success status.
CANCELLED	1	The operation was canceled (by the caller).
UNKNOWN	2	Unknown error.
INVALID_ARGUMENT	3	The client specified an invalid argument.
DEADLINE_EXCEEDED	4	The deadline expired before the operation could complete.
NOT_FOUND	5	Some requested entity was not found.
ALREADY_EXISTS	6	The entity that a client attempted to create already exists.
PERMISSION_DENIED	7	The caller does not have permission to execute the specified operation.
UNAUTHENTICATED	16	The request does not have valid authentication credentials for the operation.
RESOURCE_EXHAUSTED	8	Some resource has been exhausted.
FAILED_PRECONDITION	9	The operation was rejected because the system is not in a state required for the operation's execution.
ABORTED	10	The operation was aborted.
OUT_OF_RANGE	11	The operation was attempted past the valid range.
UNIMPLEMENTED	12	The operation is not implemented or is not supported/enabled in this service.
INTERNAL	13	Internal errors.
UNAVAILABLE	14	The service is currently unavailable.
DATA_LOSS	15	Unrecoverable data loss or corruption.

The error model provided with gRPC out of the box is quite limited and independent of the underlying gRPC data format (where the most common format is protocol buffers). If you are using protocol buffers as your data format then you can leverage the richer error model the Google APIs provide under the google.rpc package. However, the error model is supported only in the C++, Go, Java, Python, and Ruby libraries, so be mindful of this if you plan to use other languages than these.

Let's look at how these concepts can be used in a real-world gRPC error-handling use case. In our order management use case, suppose that we need to handle a request with invalid order IDs in the AddOrder remote method. As shown in Example 5-7, suppose that if the given order ID equals -1 then you need to generate an error and return it to the consumer.

Example 5-7. Error creation and propagation on the server side

```
if orderReq.Id == "-1" { ❶
    log.Printf("Order ID is invalid! -> Received Order ID %s",
        orderReq.Id)

    errorStatus := status.New(codes.InvalidArgument,
        "Invalid information received") ❷
    ds, err := errorStatus.WithDetails( ❸
        &epb.BadRequest_FieldViolation{
            Field:"ID",
            Description: fmt.Sprintf(
                "Order ID received is not valid %s : %s",
                orderReq.Id, orderReq.Description),
        },
    )
    if err != nil {
        return nil, errorStatus.Err()
    }

    return nil, ds.Err() ❹
    }
    ...
```

❶ Invalid request, needs to generate an error and send it back to the client.

❷ Create a new error status with error code `InvalidArgument`.

❸ Include any error details with an error type `BadRequest_FieldViolation` from `google.golang.org/genproto/googleapis/rpc/errdetails`.

❹ Returning the generated error.

You can simply create an error status from `grpc.status` packages with the required error code and details. In the example here we have used `status.New(codes.Invalid Argument, "Invalid information received")`. You just need to send this error back to the client with `return nil, errorStatus.Err()`. However, to include a richer error model, you can use Google API's `google.rpc` package. In this example, we have set an error detail with a specific error type from *google.golang.org/genproto/ googleapis/rpc/errdetails*.

For error handling on the client side, you simply process the error returned as part of your RPC invocation. For example, in Example 5-8, you can find the Go implementation of the client application of this order management use case. Here we invoked the AddOrder method and assigned the returned error to the `addOrderError` variable. So, the next step is to inspect the results of `addOrderError` and gracefully handle the error. For that, you can obtain the error code and specific error type that we have set from the server side.

Example 5-8. Error handling on the client side

```
order1 := pb.Order{Id: "-1",
        Items:[]string{"iPhone XS", "Mac Book Pro"},
        Destination:"San Jose, CA", Price:2300.00} ❶
res, addOrderError := client.AddOrder(ctx, &order1) ❷


if addOrderError != nil {
        errorCode := status.Code(addOrderError) ❸
        if errorCode == codes.InvalidArgument { ❹
                log.Printf("Invalid Argument Error : %s", errorCode)
                errorStatus := status.Convert(addOrderError) ❺
                for _, d := range errorStatus.Details() {
                        switch info := d.(type) {
                        case *epb.BadRequest_FieldViolation: ❻
                                log.Printf("Request Field Invalid: %s", info)
                        default:
                                log.Printf("Unexpected error type: %s", info)
                        }
                }
        } else {
                log.Printf("Unhandled error : %s ", errorCode)
        }
} else {
        log.Print("AddOrder Response -> ", res.Value)
}
```

❶ This is an invalid order.

❷ Invoke the AddOrder remote method and assign the error to addOrderError.

❸ Obtain the error code using the grpc/status package.

❹ Check for InvalidArgument error code.

❺ Obtain the error status from the error.

❻ Check for BadRequest_FieldViolation error type.

It's always good practice to use the appropriate gRPC error codes and a richer error model whenever possible for your gRPC applications. gRPC error status and details are normally sent via the trailer headers at the transport protocol level.

Now let's look at multiplexing, a service-hosting mechanism on the same gRPC server runtime.

Multiplexing

In terms of gRPC services and client applications, we've seen so far a given gRPC server with a gRPC service registered on it and a gRPC client connection being used by a single client stub only. However, gRPC allows you to run multiple gRPC services on the same gRPC server (see Figure 5-4), as well as use the same gRPC client connection for multiple gRPC client stubs. This capability is known as *multiplexing*.

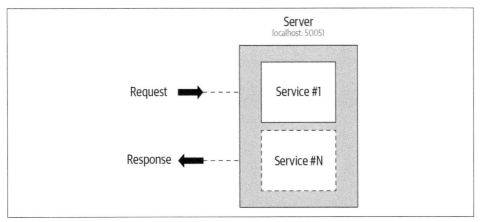

Figure 5-4. Multiplexing multiple gRPC services in the same server application

For example, in our `OrderManagement` service example, suppose that you want to run another service that is required for order-management purposes on the same gRPC server, so that the client application can reuse the same connection to invoke both the services as required. Then you can register both services on the same gRPC server by using their respective server register functions (i.e., `ordermgt_pb.RegisterOrderMa nagementServer` and `hello_pb.RegisterGreeterServer`). Using this method, you can register one or more gRPC services on the same gRPC server (as shown in Example 5-9).

Example 5-9. Two gRPC services sharing the same grpc.Server

```
func main() {
        initSampleData()
        lis, err := net.Listen("tcp", port)
        if err != nil {
                log.Fatalf("failed to listen: %v", err)
        }
        grpcServer := grpc.NewServer() ❶
```

```
// Register Order Management service on gRPC orderMgtServer
ordermgt_pb.RegisterOrderManagementServer(grpcServer, &orderMgtServer{}) ❷

// Register Greeter Service on gRPC orderMgtServer
hello_pb.RegisterGreeterServer(grpcServer, &helloServer{}) ❸

    ...
}
```

❶ Creating the gRPC server.

❷ Registering the `OrderManagement` service with the gRPC server.

❸ Registering the `Hello` service with the same gRPC server.

Similarly, from the client side you can share the same gRPC connection between two gRPC client stubs.

As shown in Example 5-10, since both gRPC services are running in the same gRPC server, you can create a gRPC connection and use it when creating the gRPC client instance for different services.

Example 5-10. Two gRPC client stubs sharing the same grpc.ClientConn

```
// Setting up a connection to the server.
conn, err := grpc.Dial(address, grpc.WithInsecure()) ❶
...

orderManagementClient := pb.NewOrderManagementClient(conn) ❷

...

// Add Order RPC
        ...
res, addErr := orderManagementClient.AddOrder(ctx, &order1)

...


helloClient := hwpb.NewGreeterClient(conn) ❸

        ...
        // Say hello RPC
helloResponse, err := helloClient.SayHello(hwcCtx,
        &hwpb.HelloRequest{Name: "gRPC Up and Running!"})
...
```

❶ Creating a gRPC connection.

❷ Using the created gRPC connection to create an OrderManagement client.

❸ Using the same gRPC connection to create the Hello service client.

Running multiple services or using the same connection between multiple stubs is a design choice that is independent of gRPC concepts. In most everyday use cases such as microservices, it is quite common to not share the same gRPC server instance between two services.

 One powerful use for gRPC multiplexing in a microservice architecture is to host multiple major versions of the same service in one server process. This allows a service to accommodate legacy clients after a breaking API change. Once the old version of the service contract is no longer in use, it can be removed from the server.

In the next section, we'll talk about how to exchange data that is not part of RPC parameters and responses between client and service applications.

Metadata

gRPC applications usually share information via RPC calls between gRPC services and consumers. In most cases, information directly related to the service's business logic and consumer is part of the remote method invocation arguments. However, in certain conditions, you may want to share information about the RPC calls that are not related to the business context of the RPC, so they shouldn't be part of the RPC arguments. In such cases, you can use *gRPC metadata* that you can send or receive from either the gRPC service or the gRPC client. As illustrated in Figure 5-5, the metadata that you create on either the client or server side can be exchanged between the client and server applications using gRPC headers. Metadata is structured in the form of a list of key(string)/value pairs.

One of the most common usages of metadata is to exchange security headers between gRPC applications. Similarly, you can use it to exchange any such information between gRPC applications. Often gRPC metadata APIs are heavily used inside the interceptors that we develop. In the next section, we'll explore how gRPC supports sending metadata between the client and server.

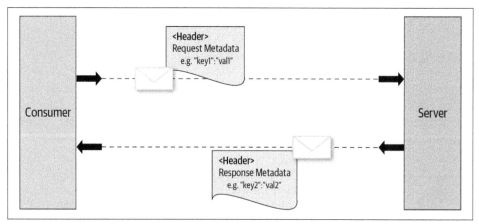

Figure 5-5. Exchanging gRPC metadata between client and server applications

Creating and Retrieving Metadata

The creation of metadata from a gRPC application is quite straightforward. In the following Go code snippet, you will find two ways of creating metadata. Metadata is represented as a normal map in Go and can be created with the format `metadata.New(map[string]string{"key1": "val1", "key2": "val2"})`. Also, you can use `metadata.Pairs` to create metadata in pairs, so that metadata with the same key will get merged into a list:

```
// Metadata Creation : option I
md := metadata.New(map[string]string{"key1": "val1", "key2": "val2"})

// Metadata Creation : option II
md := metadata.Pairs(
    "key1", "val1",
    "key1", "val1-2", // "key1" will have map value []string{"val1", "val1-2"}
    "key2", "val2",
)
```

You can also set binary data as metadata values. The binary data that we set as metadata values will be base64 encoded before sending, and will be decoded after being transferred.

Reading metadata from either the client or server side can be done using the incoming context of the RPC call with `metadata.FromIncomingContext(ctx)`, which returns the metadata map in Go:

```
func (s *server) AddOrder(ctx context.Context, orderReq *pb.Order)
    (*wrappers.StringValue, error) {

md, metadataAvailable := metadata.FromIncomingContext(ctx)
// read the required metadata from the 'md' metadata map.
```

Now let's dive into how metadata sending and receiving happens on the client or server side for different unary and streaming RPC styles.

Sending and Receiving Metadata: Client Side

You can send metadata from the client side to the gRPC service by creating metadata and setting it into the context of the RPC call. In a Go implementation, you can do this in two different ways. As shown in Example 5-11, you can create a new context with the new metadata using NewOutgoingContext, or simply append the metadata to the existing context using AppendToOutgoingContext. Using NewOutgoingContext, however, replaces any existing metadata in the context. Once you create a context with the required metadata, it can be used either for unary or streaming RPC. As you learned in Chapter 4, the metadata that you set in the context is translated into gRPC headers (on HTTP/2) or trailers at the wire level. So when the client sends those headers they are received by the recipient as headers.

Example 5-11. Sending metadata from the gRPC client side

```
md := metadata.Pairs(
        "timestamp", time.Now().Format(time.StampNano),
        "kn", "vn",
) ❶
mdCtx := metadata.NewOutgoingContext(context.Background(), md) ❷

ctxA := metadata.AppendToOutgoingContext(mdCtx,
        "k1", "v1", "k1", "v2", "k2", "v3") ❸

// make unary RPC
response, err := client.SomeRPC(ctxA, someRequest) ❹

// or make streaming RPC
stream, err := client.SomeStreamingRPC(ctxA) ❺
```

❶ Creating metadata.

❷ Creating a new context with the new metadata.

❸ Appending some more metadata to the existing context.

❹ Unary RPC using the new context with the metadata.

❺ The same context can be used for a streaming RPC, too.

Therefore, when it comes to receiving metadata from the client side, you need to treat them as either headers or trailers. In Example 5-12, you can find Go code examples on receiving metadata for both unary and streaming RPC styles.

Example 5-12. Reading metadata on the gRPC client side

```
var header, trailer metadata.MD ❶

// ***** Unary RPC *****

r, err := client.SomeRPC( ❷
    ctx,
    someRequest,
    grpc.Header(&header),
    grpc.Trailer(&trailer),
)

// process header and trailer map here.

// ***** Streaming RPC *****

stream, err := client.SomeStreamingRPC(ctx)

// retrieve header
header, err := stream.Header() ❸

// retrieve trailer
trailer := stream.Trailer() ❹

// process header and trailer map here.
```

❶ Variable to store header and trailer returned from the RPC call.

❷ Pass header and trailer reference to store the returned values for unary RPC.

❸ Getting the headers from the stream.

❹ Getting the trailers from the stream. Trailers are used to send status codes and the status message.

Once the values are obtained from the respective RPC operations, you can process them as a generic map and process the required metadata.

Now let's move on to metadata handling on the server side.

Sending and Receiving Metadata: Server Side

Receiving metadata on the server side is quite straightforward. Using Go, you can simply obtain the metadata with `metadata.FromIncomingContext(ctx)` inside your remote method implementations (see Example 5-13).

Example 5-13. Reading metadata on the gRPC server side

```go
func (s *server) SomeRPC(ctx context.Context,
    in *pb.someRequest) (*pb.someResponse, error) { ❶
    md, ok := metadata.FromIncomingContext(ctx) ❷
    // do something with metadata
}

func (s *server) SomeStreamingRPC(
    stream pb.Service_SomeStreamingRPCServer) error { ❸
    md, ok := metadata.FromIncomingContext(stream.Context()) ❹
    // do something with metadata
}
```

❶ Unary RPC.

❷ Read the metadata map from the incoming context of the remote method.

❸ Streaming RPC.

❹ Obtain the context from the stream and read metadata from it.

To send metadata from the server side, send a header with metadata or set a trailer with metadata. The metadata creation method is the same as what we discussed in the previous section. In Example 5-14, you can find Go code examples of sending metadata from a unary and a streaming remote method implementation on the server side.

Example 5-14. Sending metadata from the gRPC server side

```go
func (s *server) SomeRPC(ctx context.Context,
    in *pb.someRequest) (*pb.someResponse, error) {
    // create and send header
    header := metadata.Pairs("header-key", "val")
    grpc.SendHeader(ctx, header) ❶
    // create and set trailer
    trailer := metadata.Pairs("trailer-key", "val")
    grpc.SetTrailer(ctx, trailer) ❷
}

func (s *server) SomeStreamingRPC(stream pb.Service_SomeStreamingRPCServer) error {
    // create and send header
    header := metadata.Pairs("header-key", "val")
    stream.SendHeader(header) ❸
    // create and set trailer
    trailer := metadata.Pairs("trailer-key", "val")    stream.SetTrailer(trailer) ❹
}
```

❶ Send metadata as a header.

❷ Send metadata along with the trailer.

❸ Send metadata as a header in the stream.

❹ Send metadata along with the trailer of the stream.

In both the unary and streaming cases, you can send metadata using the grpc.Send
Header method. If you want to send metadata as part of the trailer, you need to set the
metadata as part of the trailer of the context using the grpc.SetTrailer or Set
Trailer method of the respective stream.

Now let's discuss another commonly used technique when calling gRPC applications:
name resolving.

Name Resolver

A *name resolver* takes a service name and returns a list of IPs of the backends. The
resolver used in Example 5-15 resolves lb.example.grpc.io to localhost:50051
and localhost:50052.

Example 5-15. gRPC name resolver implementation in Go

```
type exampleResolverBuilder struct{} ❶

func (*exampleResolverBuilder) Build(target resolver.Target,
        cc resolver.ClientConn,
        opts resolver.BuildOption) (resolver.Resolver, error) {

        r := &exampleResolver{ ❷
                target: target,
                cc:     cc,
                addrsStore: map[string][]string{
            exampleServiceName: addrs, ❸
                },
        }
        r.start()
        return r, nil
}
func (*exampleResolverBuilder) Scheme() string { return exampleScheme } ❹

type exampleResolver struct { ❺
        target     resolver.Target
        cc         resolver.ClientConn
        addrsStore map[string][]string
}

func (r *exampleResolver) start() {
        addrStrs := r.addrsStore[r.target.Endpoint]
```

```
        addrs := make([]resolver.Address, len(addrStrs))
        for i, s := range addrStrs {
                addrs[i] = resolver.Address{Addr: s}
        }
        r.cc.UpdateState(resolver.State{Addresses: addrs})
}
func (*exampleResolver) ResolveNow(o resolver.ResolveNowOption) {}
func (*exampleResolver) Close()                                 {}

func init() {
        resolver.Register(&exampleResolverBuilder{})
}
```

❶ Name resolver builder that creates the resolver.

❷ Creating the example resolver that resolves `lb.example.grpc.io`.

❸ This resolves `lb.example.grpc.io` to `localhost:50051` and `localhost:50052`.

❹ This resolver is created for scheme `example`.

❺ Structure of the name resolver.

Thus, based on this name resolver implementation, you can implement resolvers for any service registry of your choice such as Consul (*https://www.consul.io*), etcd (*https://etcd.io*), and Zookeeper (*https://zookeeper.apache.org*). The gRPC load-balancing requirements may be quite dependent on the deployment patterns that you use or on the use cases. With the increasing adoption of container orchestration platforms such as Kubernetes and more higher-level abstractions such as service mesh, the need to implement load-balancing logic on the client side is becoming quite rare. We'll explore some best practices for deploying gRPC applications locally on containers, as well as Kubernetes, in Chapter 7.

Now let's discuss one of the most common requirements of your gRPC applications, load balancing, in which we can use name resolvers in certain cases.

Load Balancing

Often when you develop production-ready gRPC applications, you need to make sure that your application can cater to high availability and scalability needs. Therefore, you always run more than one gRPC server in production. So, distributing RPC calls between these services needs to be taken care of by some entity. That's where load balancing comes into play. Two main load-balancing mechanisms are commonly used in gRPC: a *load-balancer (LB) proxy* and *client-side load balancing*. Let's start by discussing the LB proxy.

Load-Balancer Proxy

In proxy load balancing (Figure 5-6), the client issues RPCs to the LB proxy. Then the LB proxy distributes the RPC call to one of the available backend gRPC servers that implements the actual logic for serving the call. The LB proxy keeps track of load on each backend server and offers a different load-balancing algorithm for distributing the load among the backend services.

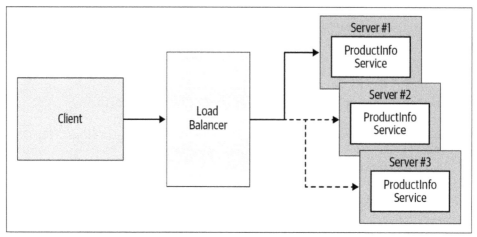

Figure 5-6. Client application invokes a load balancer that fronts multiple gRPC services

The topology of the backend services is not transparent to the gRPC clients, and they are only aware of the load balancer's endpoint. Therefore, on the client side, you don't need to make any changes to cater to a load-balancing use case, apart from using the load balancer's endpoint as the destination for all your gRPC connections. The backend services can report the load status back to the load balancer so that it can use that information for the load-balancing logic.

In theory, you can select any load balancer that supports HTTP/2 as the LB proxy for your gRPC applications. However, it must have full HTTP/2 support. Thus it's always a good idea to specifically choose load balancers that explicitly offer gRPC support. For instance, you can use load-balancing solutions such as Nginx (*https://oreil.ly/QH_1c*), Envoy proxy (*https://www.envoyproxy.io*), etc., as the LB proxy for your gRPC applications.

If you don't use a gRPC load balancer, then you can implement the load-balancing logic as part of the client applications you write. Let's look more closely at client-side load balancing.

Client-Side Load Balancing

Rather than having an intermediate proxy layer for load balancing, you can implement the load-balancing logic at the gRPC client level. In this method, the client is aware of multiple backend gRPC servers and chooses one to use for each RPC. As illustrated in Figure 5-7, the load-balancing logic may be entirely developed as part of the client application (also known as *thick client*) or it can be implemented in a dedicated server known as lookaside load balancer. Then the client can query it to obtain the best gRPC server to connect to. The client directly connects to the gRPC server address obtained by the lookaside load balancer.

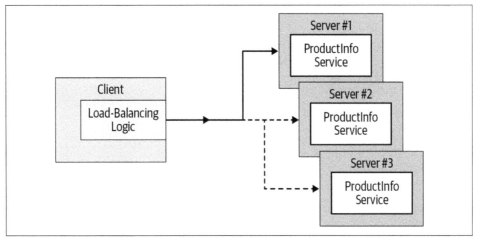

Figure 5-7. Client-side load balancing

To understand how you can implement client-side load balancing, let's look at an example of a thick client implemented using Go. In this use case, suppose we have two backend gRPC services running an echo server on :50051 and :50052. These gRPC services will include the serving address of the server as part of the RPC response. So we can consider these two servers as two members of an echo gRPC service cluster. Now, suppose we want to build a gRPC client application that uses the round-robin (executed in turn against every other) algorithm when selecting the gRPC server endpoint and another client that uses the first endpoint of the server endpoint list. Example 5-16 shows the thick client load-balancing implementation. Here you can observe that the client is dialing *example:///lb.example.grpc.io*. So, we are using the `example` scheme name and `lb.example.grpc.io` as the server name. Based on this scheme, it will look for a name resolver to discover the absolute value for the backend service address. Based on the list of values the name resolver returns, gRPC runs different load-balancing algorithms against those servers. The behavior is configured with `grpc.WithBalancerName("round_robin")`.

Example 5-16. Client-side load balancing with a thick client

```
pickfirstConn, err := grpc.Dial(
            fmt.Sprintf("%s:///%s",
    //  exampleScheme      = "example"
    //      exampleServiceName = "lb.example.grpc.io"
    exampleScheme, exampleServiceName), ❶
    // "pick_first" is the default option. ❷
            grpc.WithBalancerName("pick_first"),

            grpc.WithInsecure(),)
if err != nil {
    log.Fatalf("did not connect: %v", err)
}
defer pickfirstConn.Close()

log.Println("==== Calling helloworld.Greeter/SayHello " +
        "with pick_first ====")
makeRPCs(pickfirstConn, 10)

// Make another ClientConn with round_robin policy.
roundrobinConn, err := grpc.Dial(
    fmt.Sprintf("%s:///%s", exampleScheme, exampleServiceName),
    // "example:///lb.example.grpc.io"
    grpc.WithBalancerName("round_robin"), ❸
    grpc.WithInsecure(),
)
if err != nil {
    log.Fatalf("did not connect: %v", err)
}
defer roundrobinConn.Close()

log.Println("==== Calling helloworld.Greeter/SayHello " +
        "with round_robin ====")
makeRPCs(roundrobinConn, 10)
```

❶ Creating a gRPC connection with a *scheme* and the service name. The scheme is resolved from a scheme resolver, which is part of the client application.

❷ Specifying a load-balancing algorithm that picks the first server on the server endpoint list.

❸ Using the round-robin load-balancing algorithm.

There are two load-balancing policies supported in gRPC by default: pick_first and round_robin. pick_first tries to connect to the first address, uses it for all RPCs if it connects, or tries the next address if it fails. round_robin connects to all the addresses it sees and sends an RPC to each backend one at a time in order.

In the client-side load-balancing scenario in Example 5-16, we have a name resolver to resolve scheme `example`, which contains the logic of discovering the actual values of the endpoint URLs. Now let's talk about compression, another commonly used feature of gRPC, for sending large amounts of content over RPC.

Compression

To use network bandwidth efficiently, use compression when performing RPCs between client and services. Using gRPC compression on the client side can be implemented by setting a compressor when you do the RPC. For example, in Go, this is as easy as using `client.AddOrder(ctx, &order1, grpc.UseCompressor(gzip.Name))`, where `"google.golang.org/grpc/encoding/gzip"` provides the gzip package.

From the server side, registered compressors will be used automatically to decode request messages and encode the responses. In Go, registering a compressor is as simple as importing `"google.golang.org/grpc/encoding/gzip"` into your gRPC server application. The server always responds using the same compression method specified by the client. If the corresponding compressor has not been registered, an `Unimplemented` status will be returned to the client.

Summary

Building production-ready, real-world gRPC applications often requires you to include various capabilities besides defining the service interface, generating the server and client code, and implementing the business logic. As you saw in this chapter, gRPC offers a wide range of capabilities that you will need when building gRPC applications, including interceptors, deadlines, cancellations, and error handling.

However, we haven't yet discussed how to secure gRPC applications and how to consume them. So, in the next chapter we'll cover this topic in detail.

CHAPTER 6

Secured gRPC

gRPC-based applications communicate with each other remotely over the network. This requires each gRPC application to expose its entry point to others who need to communicate with it. From a security point of view, this is not a good thing. The more entry points we have, the broader the attack surface, and the higher the risk of being attacked. Therefore, securing communication and securing the entry points is essential for any real-world use case. Every gRPC application must be able to handle encrypted messages, encrypt all internode communications, and authenticate and sign all messages, etc.

In this chapter, we'll cover a set of security fundamentals and patterns to address the challenge we face in enabling application-level security. In simple terms, we are going to explore how we can secure communication channels between microservices and authenticate and control access by users.

So let's start with securing the communication channel.

Authenticating a gRPC Channel with TLS

Transport Level Security (TLS) aims to provide privacy and data integrity between two communicating applications. Here, it's about providing a secure connection between gRPC client and server applications. According to the Transport Level Security Protocol Specification (*https://oreil.ly/n4iIE*), when the connection between a client and a server is secure, it should have one or more of the following properties:

The connection is private

Symmetric cryptography is used for data encryption. It is a type of encryption where only one key (a secret key) is used to both encrypt and decrypt. These keys are generated uniquely for each connection based on a shared secret that was negotiated at the start of the session.

The connection is reliable
> This occurs because each message includes a message integrity check to prevent undetected loss or alteration of the data during transmission.

So it is important to send data through a secure connection. Securing gRPC connections with TLS is not a difficult task, because this authentication mechanism is built into the gRPC library. It also promotes the use of TLS to authenticate and encrypt exchanges.

How, then, do we enable transport-level security in gRPC connections? Secure data transfer between a client and server can be implemented as either one way or two way (this is also known as mutual TLS, or mTLS). In the following sections, we'll discuss how to enable security in each of these ways.

Enabling a One-Way Secured Connection

In a one-way connection, only the client validates the server to ensure that it receives data from the intended server. When establishing the connection between the client and the server, the server shares its public certificate with the client, who then validates the received certificate. This is done through a certificate authority (CA), for CA-signed certificates. Once the certificate is validated, the client sends the data encrypted using the secret key.

The CA is a trusted entity that manages and issues security certificates and public keys that are used for secure communication in a public network. Certificates signed or issued by this trusted entity are known as CA-signed certificates.

To enable TLS, first we need to create the following certificates and keys:

`server.key`
> A private RSA key to sign and authenticate the public key.

`server.pem/server.crt`
> Self-signed X.509 public keys for distribution.

> The acronym *RSA* stands for the names of three inventors: Rivest, Shamir, and Adleman. RSA is one of the most popular public-key cryptosystems, being widely used in secure data transmission. In RSA, a public key (that can be known by everyone) is used to encrypt data. A private key is then used to decrypt data. The idea is that messages encrypted with the public key can only be decrypted in a reasonable amount of time by using the private key.

To generate the keys, we can use the OpenSSL tool, which is an open source toolkit for the TLS and Secure Socket Layer (SSL) protocols. It has support for generating private keys with different sizes and pass phrases, public certificates, etc. There are other tools like mkcert (*https://mkcert.dev*) and certstrap (*https://oreil.ly/Mu4Q6*), which can also be used to generate the keys and certificates easily.

We won't describe here how to generate keys that are self-signed certificates, as step-by-step details on generating those keys and certificates are described in the README file in the source code repository.

Assume we created both a private key and public certificate. Let's use them and secure communication between the gRPC server and client for our online product management system discussed in Chapters 1 and 2.

Enabling a one-way secured connection in a gRPC server

This is the simplest way to encrypt communication between client and server. Here the server needs to be initialized with a public/private key pair. We are going to explain how it is done using our gRPC Go server.

To enable a secured Go server, let's update the main function of the server implementation, as shown in Example 6-1.

Example 6-1. gRPC secured server implementation for hosting ProductInfo service

```
package main

import (
  "crypto/tls"
  "errors"
  pb "productinfo/server/ecommerce"
  "google.golang.org/grpc"
  "google.golang.org/grpc/credentials"
  "log"
  "net"
)

var (
  port = ":50051"
  crtFile = "server.crt"
  keyFile = "server.key"
)

func main() {
  cert, err := tls.LoadX509KeyPair(crtFile,keyFile) ❶
  if err != nil {
    log.Fatalf("failed to load key pair: %s", err)
  }
  opts := []grpc.ServerOption{
    grpc.Creds(credentials.NewServerTLSFromCert(&cert)) ❷
  }

  s := grpc.NewServer(opts...) ❸
```

```
    pb.RegisterProductInfoServer(s, &server{}) ❹

    lis, err := net.Listen("tcp", port) ❺
    if err != nil {
        log.Fatalf("failed to listen: %v", err)
    }

    if err := s.Serve(lis); err != nil { ❻
        log.Fatalf("failed to serve: %v", err)
    }
}
```

❶ Read and parse a public/private key pair and create a certificate to enable TLS.

❷ Enable TLS for all incoming connections by adding certificates as TLS server credentials.

❸ Create a new gRPC server instance by passing TLS server credentials.

❹ Register the implemented service to the newly created gRPC server by calling generated APIs.

❺ Create a TCP listener on the port (50051).

❻ Bind the gRPC server to the listener and start listening to incoming messages on the port (50051).

Now we have modified the server to accept requests from clients who can verify the server certificate. Let's modify our client code to talk with this server.

Enabling a one-way secured connection in a gRPC client

In order to get the client connected, the client needs to have the server's self-certified public key. We can modify our Go client code to connect with the server as shown in Example 6-2.

Example 6-2. gRPC secured client application

```
package main

import (
  "log"

  pb "productinfo/server/ecommerce"
  "google.golang.org/grpc/credentials"
  "google.golang.org/grpc"
)
```

```
var (
  address = "localhost:50051"
  hostname = "localhost
  crtFile = "server.crt"
)

func main() {
  creds, err := credentials.NewClientTLSFromFile(crtFile, hostname) ❶
  if err != nil {
    log.Fatalf("failed to load credentials: %v", err)
  }
  opts := []grpc.DialOption{
    grpc.WithTransportCredentials(creds), ❷
  }

  conn, err := grpc.Dial(address, opts...) ❸
  if err != nil {
    log.Fatalf("did not connect: %v", err)
  }
  defer conn.Close() ❺
  c := pb.NewProductInfoClient(conn) ❹

  .... // Skip RPC method invocation.
}
```

❶ Read and parse a public certificate and create a certificate to enable TLS.

❷ Add transport credentials as a DialOption.

❸ Set up a secure connection with the server, passing dial options.

❹ Pass the connection and create a stub. This stub instance contains all the remote methods to invoke the server.

❺ Close the connection when everything is done.

This is a fairly straightforward process. We only need to add three lines and modify one from the original code. First, we create a credential object from the server public key file, then pass the transport credentials into the gRPC dialer. This will initiate the TLS handshake every time the client sets up a connection between the server.

In one-way TLS, we only authenticate server identity. Let's authenticate both parties (the client and the server) in the next section.

Enabling an mTLS Secured Connection

The main intent of an mTLS connection between client and server is to have control of clients who connect to the server. Unlike a one-way TLS connection, the server is configured to accept connections from a limited group of verified clients. Here both parties share their public certificates with each other and validate the other party. The basic flow of connection is as follows:

1. Client sends a request to access protected information from the server.
2. The server sends its X.509 certificate to the client.
3. Client validates the received certificate through a CA for CA-signed certificates.
4. If the verification is successful, the client sends its certificate to the server.
5. Server also verifies the client certificate through the CA.
6. Once it is successful, the server gives permission to access protected data.

To enable mTLS in our example, we need to figure out how to deal with client and server certificates. We need to create a CA with self-signed certificates, we need to create certificate-signing requests for both client and server, and we need to sign them using our CA. As in the previous one-way secured connection, we can use the OpenSSL tool to generate keys and certificates.

Assume we have all the required certificates to enable mTLS for client-server communication. If you generated them correctly, you will have the following keys and certificates created in your workspace:

server.key
    Private RSA key of the server.

server.crt
    Public certificate of the server.

client.key
    Private RSA key of the client.

client.crt
    Public certificate of the client.

ca.crt
    Public certificate of a CA used to sign all public certificates.

Let's first modify the server code of our example to create X.509 key pairs directly and create a certificate pool based on the CA public key.

Enabling mTLS in a gRPC server

To enable mTLS in the Go server, let's update the main function of the server implementation as shown in Example 6-3.

Example 6-3. gRPC secured server implementation for hosting ProductInfo service in Go

```go
package main

import (
  "crypto/tls"
  "crypto/x509"
  "errors"
  pb "productinfo/server/ecommerce"
  "google.golang.org/grpc"
  "google.golang.org/grpc/credentials"
  "io/ioutil"
  "log"
  "net"
)

var (
  port = ":50051"
  crtFile = "server.crt"
  keyFile = "server.key"
  caFile = "ca.crt"
)

func main() {
  certificate, err := tls.LoadX509KeyPair(crtFile, keyFile)  ❶
  if err != nil {
    log.Fatalf("failed to load key pair: %s", err)
  }

  certPool := x509.NewCertPool()  ❷
  ca, err := ioutil.ReadFile(caFile)
  if err != nil {
    log.Fatalf("could not read ca certificate: %s", err)
  }

  if ok := certPool.AppendCertsFromPEM(ca); !ok {  ❸
    log.Fatalf("failed to append ca certificate")
  }

  opts := []grpc.ServerOption{
    // Enable TLS for all incoming connections.
    grpc.Creds(  ❹
      credentials.NewTLS(&tls.Config {
        ClientAuth:   tls.RequireAndVerifyClientCert,
        Certificates: []tls.Certificate{certificate},
        ClientCAs:    certPool,
        },
      )),
  }

  s := grpc.NewServer(opts...)  ❺
  pb.RegisterProductInfoServer(s, &server{})  ❻
```

```
lis, err := net.Listen("tcp", port)  ❼
if err != nil {
    log.Fatalf("failed to listen: %v", err)
}

if err := s.Serve(lis); err != nil {  ❽
    log.Fatalf("failed to serve: %v", err)
}
}
```

❶ Create X.509 key pairs directly from the server certificate and key.

❷ Create a certificate pool from the CA.

❸ Append the client certificates from the CA to the certificate pool.

❹ Enable TLS for all incoming connections by creating TLS credentials.

❺ Create a new gRPC server instance by passing TLS server credentials.

❻ Register the gRPC service to the newly created gRPC server by calling generated APIs.

❼ Create a TCP listener on the port (50051).

❽ Bind the gRPC server to the listener and start listening to the incoming messages on the port (50051).

Now we have modified the server to accept requests from verified clients. Let's modify our client code to talk with this server.

Enabling mTLS in a gRPC client

In order to get the client connected, the client needs to follow similar steps as the server. We can modify our Go client code as shown in Example 6-4.

Example 6-4. gRPC secured client application in Go

```
package main

import (
    "crypto/tls"
    "crypto/x509"
    "io/ioutil"
    "log"

    pb "productinfo/server/ecommerce"
```

```
    "google.golang.org/grpc"
    "google.golang.org/grpc/credentials"
)



var (
    address = "localhost:50051"
    hostname = "localhost"
    crtFile = "client.crt"
    keyFile = "client.key"
    caFile = "ca.crt"
)

func main() {
    certificate, err := tls.LoadX509KeyPair(crtFile, keyFile) ❶
    if err != nil {
        log.Fatalf("could not load client key pair: %s", err)
    }

    certPool := x509.NewCertPool() ❷
    ca, err := ioutil.ReadFile(caFile)
    if err != nil {
        log.Fatalf("could not read ca certificate: %s", err)
    }

    if ok := certPool.AppendCertsFromPEM(ca); !ok { ❸
        log.Fatalf("failed to append ca certs")
    }

    opts := []grpc.DialOption{
        grpc.WithTransportCredentials( credentials.NewTLS(&tls.Config{ ❹
            ServerName:   hostname, // NOTE: this is required!
            Certificates: []tls.Certificate{certificate},
            RootCAs:      certPool,
        })),
    }

    conn, err := grpc.Dial(address, opts...) ❺
    if err != nil {
        log.Fatalf("did not connect: %v", err)
    }
    defer conn.Close()❼
    c := pb.NewProductInfoClient(conn) ❻

    .... // Skip RPC method invocation.
}
```

❶ Create X.509 key pairs directly from the server certificate and key.

❷ Create a certificate pool from the CA.

---

❸ Append the client certificates from the CA to the certificate pool.

❹ Add transport credentials as connection options. Here the `ServerName` must be equal to the `Common Name` on the certificate.

❺ Set up a secure connection with the server, passing options.

❻ Pass the connection and create a stub. This stub instance contains all the remote methods to invoke the server.

❼ Close the connection when everything is done.

Now we have secured the communication channel between the client and server of the gRPC application using both basic one-way TLS and mTLS. The next step is to enable authentication on a per-call basis, which means credentials are attached to the call. Each client call has authentication credentials and the server side checks the credentials of the call and makes a decision whether to allow the client to call or deny.

Authenticating gRPC Calls

gRPC is designed to use serious authentication mechanisms. In the previous section, we covered how to encrypt data exchanged between the client and server using TLS. Now, we're going to talk about how to verify the identity of the caller and apply access control using different call credential techniques like token-based authentication, etc.

In order to facilitate verification of the caller, gRPC provides the capability for the client to inject his or her credentials (like username and password) on every call. The gRPC server has the ability to intercept a request from the client and check these credentials for every incoming call.

First, we will review a simple authentication scenario to explain how authentication works per client call.

Using Basic Authentication

Basic authentication is the simplest authentication mechanism. In this mechanism, the client sends requests with the `Authorization` header with a value that starts with the word `Basic` followed by a space and a base64-encoded string `username:pass word`. For example, if the username is `admin` and the password is `admin`, the header value looks like this:

```
Authorization: Basic YWRtaW46YWRtaW4=
```

In general, gRPC doesn't encourage us to use a username/password for authenticating to services. This is because a username/password doesn't have control in time as opposed to other tokens (JSON Web Tokens [JWTs], OAuth2 access tokens). This means when we generate a token, we can specify how long it is valid. But for a username/password, we cannot specify a validity period. It is valid until we change the password. If you need to enable basic authentication in your application, it's advised that you share basic credentials in a secure connection between client and server. We pick basic authentication because it is easier to explain how authentication works in gRPC.

Let's first discuss how to inject user credentials (in basic authentication) into the call. Since there is no built-in support for basic authentication in gRPC, we need to add it as custom credentials to the client context. In Go, we can easily do this by defining a credential struct and implementing the PerRPCCredentials interface as shown in Example 6-5.

Example 6-5. Implement PerRPCCredentials interface to pass custom credentials

```
type basicAuth struct { ❶
  username string
  password string
}

func (b basicAuth) GetRequestMetadata(ctx context.Context,
  in ...string)  (map[string]string, error) { ❷
  auth := b.username + ":" + b.password
  enc := base64.StdEncoding.EncodeToString([]byte(auth))
  return map[string]string{
     "authorization": "Basic " + enc,
  }, nil
}

func (b basicAuth) RequireTransportSecurity() bool { ❸
  return true
}
```

❶ Define a struct to hold the collection on fields you want to inject in your RPC calls (in our case, it is user credentials like username and password).

❷ Implement the GetRequestMetadata method and convert user credentials to request metadata. In our case, "Authorization" is the key and the value is "Basic" followed by base64 (<username>:<password>).

❸ Specify whether channel security is required to pass these credentials. As mentioned earlier, it is advisable to use channel security.

Once we implement a credentials object, we need to initiate it with valid credentials and pass it when creating the connection as shown in Example 6-6.

Example 6-6. gRPC secured client application with basic authentication

```go
package main

import (
  "log"
  pb "productinfo/server/ecommerce"
  "google.golang.org/grpc/credentials"
  "google.golang.org/grpc"
)

var (
  address = "localhost:50051"
  hostname = "localhost"
  crtFile = "server.crt"
)

func main() {
  creds, err := credentials.NewClientTLSFromFile(crtFile, hostname)
  if err != nil {
    log.Fatalf("failed to load credentials: %v", err)
  }

  auth := basicAuth{  ❶
    username: "admin",
    password: "admin",
  }

  opts := []grpc.DialOption{
    grpc.WithPerRPCCredentials(auth),  ❷
    grpc.WithTransportCredentials(creds),
  }

  conn, err := grpc.Dial(address, opts...)
  if err != nil {
    log.Fatalf("did not connect: %v", err)
  }
  defer conn.Close()
  c := pb.NewProductInfoClient(conn)

  .... // Skip RPC method invocation.
}
```

❶ Initialize the auth variable with valid user credentials (username and password). The auth variable holds the values we are going to use.

❷ Pass the auth variable to the grpc.WithPerRPCCredentials function. The grpc.WithPerRPCCredentials() function takes an interface as a parameter. Since we define our authentication structure to comply with the interface, we can pass our variable.

Now the client is pushing extra metadata during its calls to the server, but the server does not care. So we need to tell the server to check metadata. Let's update our server to read the metadata as shown in Example 6-7.

Example 6-7. gRPC secured server with basic user credential validation

```go
package main

import (
  "context"
  "crypto/tls"
  "encoding/base64"
  "errors"
  pb "productinfo/server/ecommerce"
  "google.golang.org/grpc"
  "google.golang.org/grpc/codes"
  "google.golang.org/grpc/credentials"
  "google.golang.org/grpc/metadata"
  "google.golang.org/grpc/status"
  "log"
  "net"
  "path/filepath"
  "strings"
)


var (
  port = ":50051"
  crtFile = "server.crt"
  keyFile = "server.key"
  errMissingMetadata = status.Errorf(codes.InvalidArgument, "missing metadata")
  errInvalidToken    = status.Errorf(codes.Unauthenticated, "invalid credentials")
)

type server struct {
  productMap map[string]*pb.Product
}


func main() {
  cert, err := tls.LoadX509KeyPair(crtFile, keyFile)
  if err != nil {
    log.Fatalf("failed to load key pair: %s", err)
  }
  opts := []grpc.ServerOption{
    // Enable TLS for all incoming connections.
    grpc.Creds(credentials.NewServerTLSFromCert(&cert)),

    grpc.UnaryInterceptor(ensureValidBasicCredentials), ❶
  }
```

```
  s := grpc.NewServer(opts...)
  pb.RegisterProductInfoServer(s, &server{})

  lis, err := net.Listen("tcp", port)
  if err != nil {
     log.Fatalf("failed to listen: %v", err)
  }

  if err := s.Serve(lis); err != nil {
     log.Fatalf("failed to serve: %v", err)
  }
}

func valid(authorization []string) bool {
  if len(authorization) < 1 {
     return false
  }
  token := strings.TrimPrefix(authorization[0], "Basic ")
  return token == base64.StdEncoding.EncodeToString([]byte("admin:admin"))
}

func ensureValidBasicCredentials(ctx context.Context, req interface{}, info
*grpc.UnaryServerInfo,
     handler grpc.UnaryHandler) (interface{}, error) { ❷
  md, ok := metadata.FromIncomingContext(ctx) ❸
  if !ok {
     return nil, errMissingMetadata
  }
  if !valid(md["authorization"]) {
     return nil, errInvalidToken
  }
  // Continue execution of handler after ensuring a valid token.
  return handler(ctx, req)
}
```

❶ Add a new server option (grpc.ServerOption) with the TLS server certificate. grpc.UnaryInterceptor is a function where we add an interceptor to intercept all requests from the client. We pass a reference to a function (ensureValidBasic Credentials) so the interceptor passes all client requests to that function.

❷ Define a function called ensureValidBasicCredentials to validate caller identity. Here, the context.Context object contains the metadata we need and that will exist during the lifetime of the request.

❸ Extract the metadata from the context, get the value of the authentication, and validate the credentials. The keys within metadata.MD are normalized to lowercase. So we need to check the value for the lowercase key.

Now the server is validating client identity in each call. This is a very simple example. You can have complex authentication logic inside the server interceptor to validate client identity.

Since you have a basic understanding of how client authentication works, per request, let's talk about commonly used and recommended token-based authentication (OAuth 2.0).

Using OAuth 2.0

OAuth 2.0 (*https://oauth.net/2*) is a framework for access delegation. It allows users to grant limited access to services on their behalf, rather than giving them total access like with a username and password. Here we are not going to discuss OAuth 2.0 in detail. It is helpful if you have some basic knowledge about how OAuth 2.0 works to enable it in your application.

In the OAuth 2.0 flow, there are four main characters: the client, the authorization server, the resource server, and the resource owner. The *client* wants to access the resource in a resource server. To access the resource, the client needs to get a token (which is an arbitrary string) from the *authorization server*. This token must be of a proper length and should not be predictable. Once the client receives the token, the client can send a request to the *resource server* with the token. The resource server then talks to the corresponding authorization server and validates the token. If it is validated by this *resource owner*, the client can access the resource.

gRPC has built-in support to enable OAuth 2.0 in a gRPC application. Let's first discuss how to inject a token into the call. Since we don't have an authorization server in our example, we are going to hardcode an arbitrary string for the token value. Example 6-8 illustrates how to add an OAuth token to a client request.

Example 6-8. gRPC secured client application with OAuth token in Go

```
package main

import (
  "google.golang.org/grpc/credentials"
  "google.golang.org/grpc/credentials/oauth"
  "log"

  pb "productinfo/server/ecommerce"
  "golang.org/x/oauth2"
  "google.golang.org/grpc"
)
```

```go
var (
    address  = "localhost:50051"
    hostname = "localhost"
    crtFile  = "server.crt"
)

func main() {
    auth := oauth.NewOauthAccess(fetchToken())  ❶

    creds, err := credentials.NewClientTLSFromFile(crtFile, hostname)
    if err != nil {
        log.Fatalf("failed to load credentials: %v", err)
    }

    opts := []grpc.DialOption{
        grpc.WithPerRPCCredentials(auth),  ❷
        grpc.WithTransportCredentials(creds),
    }

    conn, err := grpc.Dial(address, opts...)
    if err != nil {
        log.Fatalf("did not connect: %v", err)
    }
    defer conn.Close()
    c := pb.NewProductInfoClient(conn)

    .... // Skip RPC method invocation.
}

func fetchToken() *oauth2.Token {
    return &oauth2.Token{
        AccessToken: "some-secret-token",
    }
}
```

❶ Set up the credentials for the connection. We need to provide an OAuth2 token value to create the credentials. Here we use a hardcoded string value for the token.

❷ Configure gRPC dial options to apply a single OAuth token for all RPC calls on the same connection. If you want to apply an OAuth token per call, then you need to configure the gRPC call with CallOption.

Note that we also enable channel security because OAuth requires the underlying transport to be secure. Inside gRPC, the provided token is prefixed with the token type and attached to the metadata with the key authorization.

In the server, we add a similar interceptor to check and validate the client token that comes with the request as shown in Example 6-9.

Example 6-9. gRPC secured server with OAuth user token validation

```go
package main

import (
  "context"
  "crypto/tls"
  "errors"
  "log"
  "net"
  "strings"

  pb "productinfo/server/ecommerce"
  "google.golang.org/grpc"
  "google.golang.org/grpc/codes"
  "google.golang.org/grpc/credentials"
  "google.golang.org/grpc/metadata"
  "google.golang.org/grpc/status"
)

// server is used to implement ecommerce/product_info.
type server struct {
  productMap map[string]*pb.Product
}

var (
  port = ":50051"
  crtFile = "server.crt"
  keyFile = "server.key"
  errMissingMetadata = status.Errorf(codes.InvalidArgument, "missing metadata")
  errInvalidToken    = status.Errorf(codes.Unauthenticated, "invalid token")
)

func main() {
  cert, err := tls.LoadX509KeyPair(crtFile, keyFile)
  if err != nil {
    log.Fatalf("failed to load key pair: %s", err)
  }
  opts := []grpc.ServerOption{
    grpc.Creds(credentials.NewServerTLSFromCert(&cert)),
    grpc.UnaryInterceptor(ensureValidToken), ❶
  }

  s := grpc.NewServer(opts...)
  pb.RegisterProductInfoServer(s, &server{})

  lis, err := net.Listen("tcp", port)
  if err != nil {
    log.Fatalf("failed to listen: %v", err)
  }

  if err := s.Serve(lis); err != nil {
```

```
    log.Fatalf("failed to serve: %v", err)
  }
}

func valid(authorization []string) bool {
  if len(authorization) < 1 {
    return false
  }
  token := strings.TrimPrefix(authorization[0], "Bearer ")
  return token == "some-secret-token"
}

func ensureValidToken(ctx context.Context, req interface{}, info *grpc.UnaryServerInfo,
    handler grpc.UnaryHandler) (interface{}, error) { ❷
  md, ok := metadata.FromIncomingContext(ctx)
  if !ok {
    return nil, errMissingMetadata
  }
  if !valid(md["authorization"]) {
    return nil, errInvalidToken
  }
  return handler(ctx, req)
}
```

❶   Add the new server option (grpc.ServerOption) along with the TLS server certificate. With the grpc.UnaryInterceptor function, we add an interceptor to intercept all requests from the client.

❷   Define a function called ensureValidToken to validate the token. If the token is missing or invalid, the interceptor blocks the execution and gives an error. Otherwise, the interceptor invokes the next handler passing the context and interface.

It is possible to configure token validation for all RPCs using an interceptor. A server may configure either a grpc.UnaryInterceptor or a grpc.StreamInterceptor depending on the service type.

Similar to OAuth 2.0 authentication, gRPC also supports JSON Web Token (JWT)-based authentication. In the next section, we'll discuss what changes we need to make to enable JWT-based authentication.

Using JWT

JWT defines a container to transport identity information between the client and server. A signed JWT can be used as a self-contained access token, which means the resource server doesn't need to talk to the authentication server to validate the client token. It can validate the token by validating the signature. The client requests access from the authentication server, which verifies the client's credentials, creates a JWT, and sends it to the client. The client application with JWT allows access to resources.

gRPC has built-in support for JWT. If you have the JWT file from the authentication server, you need to pass that token file and create JWT credentials. The code snippet in Example 6-10 illustrates how to create JWT credentials from the JWT token file (*token.json*) and pass them as `DialOptions` in a Go client application.

Example 6-10. Setting up a connection using a JWT in a Go client application

```
jwtCreds, err := oauth.NewJWTAccessFromFile("token.json")  ❶
if err != nil {
  log.Fatalf("Failed to create JWT credentials: %v", err)
}

creds, err := credentials.NewClientTLSFromFile("server.crt",
     "localhost")
if err != nil {
   log.Fatalf("failed to load credentials: %v", err)
}
opts := []grpc.DialOption{
  grpc.WithPerRPCCredentials(jwtCreds),
  // transport credentials.
  grpc.WithTransportCredentials(creds),  ❷
}

// Set up a connection to the server.
conn, err := grpc.Dial(address, opts...)
if err != nil {
  log.Fatalf("did not connect: %v", err)
}
   .... // Skip Stub generation and RPC method invocation.
```

❶ Call `oauth.NewJWTAccessFromFile` to initialize a `credentials.PerRPCCreden tials`. We need to provide a valid token file to create the credentials.

❷ Configure a gRPC dial with `DialOption` `WithPerRPCCredentials` to apply a JWT token for all RPC calls on the same connection.

In addition to these authentication techniques, we can add any authentication mechanism by extending RPC credentials on the client side and adding a new interceptor on the server side. gRPC also provides special built-in support for calling gRPC services deployed in Google Cloud. in the next section, we'll discuss how to call those services.

Using Google Token-Based Authentication

Identifying the users and deciding whether to let them use the services deployed on the Google Cloud Platform is controlled by the Extensible Service Proxy (ESP). ESP supports multiple authentication methods, including Firebase, Auth0, and Google ID tokens. In each case, the client needs to provide a valid JWT in their requests. In order to generate authenticating JWTs, we must create a service account for each deployed service.

Once we have the JWT token for the service, we can call the service method by sending the token along with the request. We can create the channel passing the credentials as shown in Example 6-11.

Example 6-11. Setting up a connection with a Google endpoint in a Go client application

```
perRPC, err := oauth.NewServiceAccountFromFile("service-account.json", scope) ❶
if err != nil {
  log.Fatalf("Failed to create JWT credentials: %v", err)
}

pool, _ := x509.SystemCertPool()
creds := credentials.NewClientTLSFromCert(pool, "")

opts := []grpc.DialOption{
  grpc.WithPerRPCCredentials(perRPC),
  grpc.WithTransportCredentials(creds), ❷
}

conn, err := grpc.Dial(address, opts...)
if err != nil {
  log.Fatalf("did not connect: %v", err)
}
.... // Skip Stub generation and RPC method invocation.
```

❶ Call oauth.NewServiceAccountFromFile to initialize credentials.PerRPCCre dentials. We need to provide a valid token file to create the credentials.

❷ Similar to authentication mechanisms discussed earlier, we configure a gRPC dial with DialOption WithPerRPCCredentials to apply the authentication token as metadata for all RPC calls on the same connection.

Summary

When building a production-ready gRPC application, it is essential to have at least minimum security requirements for the gRPC application to ensure secure communication between the client and server. The gRPC library is designed to work with different kinds of authentication mechanisms and capable of extending support by adding a custom authentication mechanism. This makes it easy to safely use gRPC to talk to other systems.

There are two types of credential supports in gRPC, channel and call. Channel credentials are attached to the channels such as TLS, etc. Call credentials are attached to the call, such as OAuth 2.0 tokens, basic authentication, etc. We even can apply both credential types to the gRPC application. For example, we can have TLS enable the connection between client and server and also attach credentials to each RPC call made on the connection.

In this chapter, you learned how to enable both credential types to your gRPC application. In the next chapter, we'll expand on the concepts and technologies you've learned to build and run real-world gRPC applications in production. We'll also discuss how to write test cases for service and client applications, how to deploy an application on Docker and Kubernetes, and how to observe the system when it runs in production.

CHAPTER 7

Running gRPC in Production

In previous chapters, we focused on various aspects of designing and developing gRPC-based applications. Now, it's time to dive into the details of running gRPC applications in production. In this chapter, we'll discuss how you can develop unit testing or integration testing for your gRPC services and client as well as how you can integrate them with continuous integration tools. Then we'll move into the continuous deployment of a gRPC application where we explore some deployment patterns on virtual machines (VMs), Docker, and Kubernetes. Finally, to operate your gRPC applications in production environments, you need to have a solid observability platform. This is where we will discuss different observability tools for gRPC applications and explore troubleshooting and debugging techniques for gRPC applications. Let's begin our discussion with testing these applications.

Testing gRPC Applications

Any software application that you develop (including gRPC applications) needs to have associated unit testing along with the application. As gRPC applications always interact with the network, the testing should also cover the network RPC aspect of both the server and client gRPC applications. We'll start by testing the gRPC server.

Testing a gRPC Server

gRPC service testing is often done using a gRPC client application as part of the test cases. The server-side testing consists of starting a gRPC server with the required gRPC service and then connecting to the server using the client application where you implement your test cases. Let's take a look at a sample test case written for the Go implementation of our ProductInfo service. In Go, the implementation of the gRPC test case should be implemented as a generic test case of Go using the testing package (see Example 7-1).

Example 7-1. gRPC server-side test using Go

```
func TestServer_AddProduct(t *testing.T) { ❶
        grpcServer := initGRPCServerHTTP2() ❷
        conn, err := grpc.Dial(address, grpc.WithInsecure()) ❸
        if err != nil {

            grpcServer.Stop()
            t.Fatalf("did not connect: %v", err)
        }
        defer conn.Close()
        c := pb.NewProductInfoClient(conn)

        name := "Sumsung S10"
        description := "Samsung Galaxy S10 is the latest smart phone, launched in
        February 2019"
        price := float32(700.0)
        ctx, cancel := context.WithTimeout(context.Background(), time.Second)
        defer cancel()
        r, err := c.AddProduct(ctx, &pb.Product{Name: name,
                                    Description: description, Price: price}) ❹
        if err != nil { ❺
                t.Fatalf("Could not add product: %v", err)
        }

        if r.Value == "" {
                t.Errorf("Invalid Product ID %s", r.Value)
        }
        log.Printf("Res %s", r.Value)
    grpcServer.Stop()
}
```

❶ Conventional test that starts a gRPC server and client to test the service with RPC.

❷ Starting a conventional gRPC server running on HTTP/2.

❸ Connecting to the server application.

❹ Sends RPC for `AddProduct` method.

❺ Verification of the response message.

As gRPC test cases are based on standard language test cases, the way in which you execute them will not be different from a standard test case. One special thing about the server-side gRPC tests is that they require the server application to open up a port the client application connects to. If you prefer not to do this, or your testing environment doesn't allow it, you can use a library to help avoid starting up a service with a real port number. In Go, you can use the bufconn package (*https://oreil.ly/gOq46*), which provides a `net.Conn` implemented by a buffer and related dialing and listening functionality. You can find the full code sample in the source code repository for this chapter. If you are using Java you can use a test framework such as *JUnit* and follow the exact same procedure to write a server-side gRPC test. However, if you prefer to write the test case without starting a gRPC server instance, then you can use the gRPC in-process server of the Java implementation. You can find a complete Java code example for this in the code repository of this book.

It is also possible to unit test the business logic of the remote functions that you develop without going through the RPC network layer. You can instead directly test the functions by invoking them without using a gRPC client.

With this, we have learned how to write tests for gRPC services. Now let's talk about how to test your gRPC client applications.

Testing a gRPC Client

When we are developing tests for a gRPC client, one of the possible approaches to testing would be to start a gRPC server and implement a mock service. However, this won't be a very straightforward task as it will have the overhead of opening a port and connecting to a server. Therefore, to test client-side logic without the overhead of connecting to a real server, you can use a mocking framework. Mocking of the gRPC server side enables developers to write lightweight unit tests to check functionalities on the client side without invoking RPC calls to a server.

If you are developing a gRPC client application with Go, you can use Gomock (*https://oreil.ly/8GAWB*) to mock the client interface (using the generated code) and programmatically set its methods to expect and return predetermined values. Using Gomock, you can generate mock interfaces for the gRPC client application using:

```
mockgen github.com/grpc-up-and-running/samples/ch07/grpc-docker/go/proto-gen \
ProductInfoClient > mock_prodinfo/prodinfo_mock.go
```

Here, we've specified `ProductInfoClient` as the interface to be mocked. Then the test code you write can import the package generated by `mockgen` along with the `gomock` package to write unit tests around client-side logic. As shown in Example 7-2, you can create a mock object to expect a call to its method and return a response.

Example 7-2. gRPC client-side test with Gomock

```
func TestAddProduct(t *testing.T) {
        ctrl := gomock.NewController(t)
        defer ctrl.Finish()
        mocklProdInfoClient := NewMockProductInfoClient(ctrl) ❶
    ...
        req := &pb.Product{Name: name, Description: description, Price: price}
```

```
      mocklProdInfoClient. ❷
        EXPECT().AddProduct(gomock.Any(), &rpcMsg{msg: req},).  ❸
        Return(&wrapper.StringValue{Value: "ABC123" + name}, nil)  ❹

      testAddProduct(t, mocklProdInfoClient)  ❺
}

func testAddProduct(t *testing.T, client pb.ProductInfoClient) {
      ctx, cancel := context.WithTimeout(context.Background(), time.Second)
      defer cancel()
      ...

      r, err := client.AddProduct(ctx, &pb.Product{Name: name,
   Description: description, Price: price})

      // test and verify response.
}
```

❶ Creating a mock object to expect calls to remote methods.

❷ Programming the mock object.

❸ Expect a call to the AddProduct method.

❹ Return a mock value for product ID.

❺ Call the actual test method that invokes the remote method of the client stub.

If you are using Java, you can test the client application using Mockito (*https:// site.mockito.org*) and the in-process server implementation for the Java implementation of gRPC. You can refer to the source code repository for more details of these samples. Once you have the required server- and client-side testing in place you can integrate them with the continuous integration tools that you use.

It is important to keep in mind that mocking gRPC servers will not give you the exact same behavior as with a real gRPC server. So certain capabilities may not be able to be verified via test unless you re-implement all the error logic present in gRPC servers. In practice, you can verify a selected set of capabilities via mocking and the rest needs to be verified against the actual gRPC server implementation. Now let's look at how you can do load testing and benchmarking of your gRPC applications.

Load Testing

It is difficult to conduct load testing and benchmarking for gRPC applications using conventional tools, as these applications are more or less bound to specific protocols such as HTTP. Therefore, for gRPC we need tailor-made load-testing tools that can load test the gRPC server by generating a virtual load of RPCs to the server.

---

ghz (*https://ghz.sh*) is such a load-testing tool; it is implemented as a command-line utility using Go. It can be used for testing and debugging services locally, and also in automated continuous integration environments for performance regression testing. For example, using ghz you can run a load test with the following command:

```
ghz --insecure \
  --proto ./greeter.proto \
  --call helloworld.Greeter.SayHello \
  -d '{"name":"Joe"}'\
  -n 2000 \
  -c 20 \

  0.0.0.0:50051
```

Here we invoke a SayHello remote method of the Greeter service insecurely. We can specify the total number of requests (-n 2000) and concurrency (20 threads). The results can also be generated in various output formats.

Once you have the required server- and client-side testing in place, you can integrate them with the continuous integration tools that you use.

Continuous Integration

If you are new to *continuous integration* (CI), it is a development practice that requires developers to frequently integrate code into a shared repository. During each check-in the code is then verified by an automated build, allowing teams to detect problems early. When it comes to gRPC applications, often the server- and client-side applications are independent and may be built with disparate technologies. So, as part of the CI process, you will have to verify the gRPC client- or server-side code using the unit and integration testing techniques that we learned in the previous section. Then based on the language that you use to build the gRPC application, you can integrate the testing (e.g., Go testing or Java JUnit) of those applications with the CI tool of your choice. For instance, if you have written tests using Go, then you can easily integrate your Go tests with tools such as Jenkins (*https://jenkins.io*), TravisCI (*https://travis-ci.com*), Spinnaker (*https://www.spinnaker.io*), etc.

Once you establish a testing and CI procedure for your gRPC application, the next thing that you need to look into is the deployment of your gRPC applications.

Deployment

Now, let's look into the different deployment methods for the gRPC applications that we develop. If you intend to run a gRPC server or client application locally or on VMs, the deployment merely depends on the binaries that you generate for the corresponding programming language of your gRPC application. For local or VM-based deployment, the scaling and high availability of gRPC server applications is usually achieved using standard deployment practices such as using load balancers that support the gRPC protocol.

Most modern applications are now deployed as containers. Therefore, it's quite useful to take a look at how you can deploy your gRPC applications on containers. Docker is the standard platform for container-based application deployment.

Deploying on Docker

Docker (*https://www.docker.com*) is an open platform for developing, shipping, and running applications. Using Docker, you can separate your applications from your infrastructure. It offers the ability to package and run an application in an isolated environment called a *container* so that you can run multiple containers on the same host. Containers are much more lightweight than conventional VMs and run directly within the host machine's kernel.

Let's look at some examples of deploying a gRPC application as a Docker container.

 The fundamentals of Docker are beyond the scope of this book. Hence, we recommend you refer to the Docker documentation (*https://docs.docker.com*) and other resources if you are not familiar with Docker.

Once you develop a gRPC server application, you can create a Docker container for it. Example 7-3 shows a Dockerfile of a Go-based gRPC server. There are many gRPC-specific constructs in the Dockerfile. In this example, we have used a multistage Docker build where we build the application in stage 1, and then run the application in stage 2 as a much more lightweight runtime. The generated server-side code is also added into the container prior to building the application.

Example 7-3. Dockerfile for Go gRPC server

```
# Multistage build

# Build stage I: ❶
FROM golang AS build
ENV location /go/src/github.com/grpc-up-and-running/samples/ch07/grpc-docker/go
WORKDIR ${location}/server

ADD ./server ${location}/server
ADD ./proto-gen ${location}/proto-gen

RUN go get -d ./... ❷
RUN go install ./... ❸

RUN CGO_ENABLED=0 go build -o /bin/grpc-productinfo-server ❹
```

```
# Build stage II: ❺
FROM scratch
COPY --from=build /bin/grpc-productinfo-server /bin/grpc-productinfo-server ❻

ENTRYPOINT ["/bin/grpc-productinfo-server"]
EXPOSE 50051
```

❶ Only the Go language and Alpine Linux is needed to build the program.

❷ Download all the dependencies.

❸ Install all the packages.

❹ Building the server application.

❺ Go binaries are self-contained executables.

❻ Copy the binary that we built in the previous stage to the new location.

Once you create the Dockerfile you can build the Docker image using:

```
docker image build -t grpc-productinfo-server -f server/Dockerfile
```

The gRPC client application can be created using the same approach. One exception here is that, since we are running our server application on Docker, the hostname and port that the client application uses to connect to gRPC is now different.

When we run both the server and client gRPC applications on Docker, they need to communicate with each other and the outside world via the host machine. So there has to be a layer of networking involved. Docker supports different types of networks, each fit for certain use cases. So, when we run the server and client Docker containers, we can specify a common network so that the client application can discover the location of the server application based on the hostname. This means that the client application code has to change so that it connects to the hostname of the server. For example, our Go gRPC application must be modified to call the service hostname instead of localhost:

```
conn, err := grpc.Dial("productinfo:50051", grpc.WithInsecure())
```

You may read the hostname from the environment rather than hardcoding it in your client application. Once you are done with the changes to the client application, you need to rebuild the Docker image and then run both the server and client images as shown here:

```
docker run -it --network=my-net --name=productinfo \
    --hostname=productinfo
    -p 50051:50051  grpc-productinfo-server ❶
```

```
docker run -it --network=my-net \
    --hostname=client grpc-productinfo-client ❷
```

❶ Running the gRPC server with hostname `productinfo`, port 50051 on Docker
network *my-net*.

❷ Running the gRPC client on Docker network *my-net*.

When starting Docker containers, you can specify a Docker network that a given
container runs on. If the service shares the same network, then the client application
can discover the actual address of the host service using the hostname provided along
with the `docker run` command.

When the number of containers you run is small and their interactions are relatively
simple, then you can possibly build your solution entirely on Docker. However, most
real-world scenarios require the management of multiple containers and their interactions. Building such solutions solely based on Docker is quite tedious. That's where
a container orchestration platform comes into the picture.

Deploying on Kubernetes

Kubernetes is an open source platform for automating deployment, scaling, and management of containerized applications. When you run a containerized gRPC application using Docker, there's no scalability or high-availability guarantee provided out of
the box. You need to build those things outside the Docker containers. Kubernetes
provides a wide range of such capabilities, so that you can offload most container-
management and orchestration tasks to the underlying Kubernetes platform.

Kubernetes (*https://kubernetes.io*) provides a reliable and scalable
platform for running containerized workloads. Kubernetes takes
care of scaling requirements, failover, service, discovery, configuration management, security, deployment patterns, and much more.

The fundamentals of Kubernetes are beyond the scope of this book.
Hence, we recommend that you refer to the Kubernetes documentation (*https://oreil.ly/csW_8*) and other such resources to learn
more.

Let's look at how your gRPC server application can be deployed into Kubernetes.

Kubernetes deployment resource for a gRPC server

To deploy in Kubernetes, the first thing you need to do is create a Docker container
for your gRPC server application. We did exactly this in the previous section, and you
can use the same container here. You can push the container image to a container
registry such as Docker Hub.

For this example, we have pushed the gRPC server Docker image to Docker Hub under the tag `kasunindrasiri/grpc-productinfo-server`. The Kubernetes platform doesn't directly manage containers, rather, it uses an abstraction called *pods*. A pod is a logical unit that may contain one or more containers; it is the unit of replication in Kubernetes. For example, if you need multiple instances of the gRPC server application, then Kubernetes will create more pods. The containers running on a given pod share the same resources and local network. However, in our case, we only need to run a gRPC server container in our pod. So, it's a pod with a single container. Kubernetes doesn't manage pods directly. Rather, it uses another abstraction called a *deployment*. A deployment specifies the number of pods that should be running at a time. When a new deployment is created, Kubernetes spins up the number of pods specified in the deployment.

To deploy our gRPC server application in Kubernetes, we need to create a Kubernetes deployment using the YAML descriptor shown in Example 7-4.

Example 7-4. Kubernetes deployment descriptor of a Go gRPC server application

```yaml
apiVersion: apps/v1
kind: Deployment ❶
metadata:
  name: grpc-productinfo-server ❷
spec:
  replicas: 1 ❸
  selector:
    matchLabels:
      app: grpc-productinfo-server
  template:
    metadata:
      labels:
        app: grpc-productinfo-server
    spec:
      containers:
      - name: grpc-productinfo-server ❹
        image: kasunindrasiri/grpc-productinfo-server ❺
        resources:
          limits:
            memory: "128Mi"
            cpu: "500m"
        ports:
        - containerPort: 50051
          name: grpc
```

❶ Declaring a Kubernetes `Deployment` object.

❷ Name of the deployment.

❸ Number of gRPC server pods that should be running at a time.

❹ Name of the associated gRPC server container.

❺ Image name and tag of the gRPC server container.

When you apply this descriptor in Kubernetes using `kubectl apply -f server/`
`grpc-prodinfo-server.yaml`, you get a Kubernetes deployment of one gRPC server
pod running in your Kubernetes cluster. However, if the gRPC client application has
to access a gRPC server pod running in the same Kubernetes cluster, it has to find out
the exact IP address and port of the pod and send the RPC. However, the IP address
may change when the pod gets restarted, and if you are running multiple replicas you
have to deal with multiple IP addresses of each replica. To overcome this limitation,
Kubernetes provides an abstraction called a *service*.

Kubernetes service resource for a gRPC server

You can create a Kubernetes service and associate it with the matching pods (gRPC
server pods in this case) and you will get a DNS name that will automatically route
the traffic to any matching pod. So, you can think of a service as a web proxy or a
load balancer that forwards the requests to the underlying pods. Example 7-5 shows
the Kubernetes service descriptor for the gRPC server application.

Example 7-5. Kubernetes service descriptor of a Go gRPC server application

```
apiVersion: v1
kind: Service ❶
metadata:
  name: productinfo ❷
spec:
  selector:
    app: grpc-productinfo-server ❸
  ports:
  - port: 50051 ❹
    targetPort: 50051
    name: grpc
  type: NodePort
```

❶ Specifying a `Service` descriptor.

❷ Name of the service. This will be used by the client application when connecting
to the service.

❸ This tells the service to route requests to the pods for matching label `grpc-`
`productinfo-server`.

---

❹ Service runs on port 50051 and forwards the requests to target port 50051.

So, once you have created both the Deployment and Service descriptor, you can deploy this application into Kubernetes using kubectl apply -f server/grpc-prodinfo-server.yaml (you can have both descriptors in the same YAML file). A successful deployment of these objects should give you a running gRPC server pod, a Kubernetes service for a gRPC server, and a deployment.

The next step is deploying the gRPC client into Kubernetes cluster.

Kubernetes Job for running a gRPC Client

When you have the gRPC server up and running on the Kubernetes cluster, then you can also run the gRPC client application in the same cluster. The client can access the gRPC server via the gRPC service productinfo that we created in the previous step. So from the client's code, you should refer to the Kubernetes service name as the hostname and use the service port as the port name of the gRPC server. Therefore, the client will be using grpc.Dial("productinfo:50051", grpc.WithInsecure()) when connecting to the server in the Go implementation of the client. If we assume that our client application needs to run a specified number of times (i.e., just calls the gRPC service, logs the response, and exits), then rather than using a Kubernetes Deployment, we may use a Kubernetes *job*. A Kubernetes job is designed to run a Pod a specified number of times.

You can create the client application container the same way we did in the gRPC server. Once you have the container pushed into the Docker registry, then you can specify the Kubernetes Job descriptor as shown in Example 7-6.

Example 7-6. gRPC client application runs as a Kubernetes job

```
apiVersion: batch/v1
kind: Job ❶
metadata:
  name: grpc-productinfo-client ❷
spec:
  completions: 1 ❸
  parallelism: 1 ❹
  template:
    spec:
      containers:
      - name: grpc-productinfo-client ❺
        image: kasunindrasiri/grpc-productinfo-client ❻
      restartPolicy: Never
  backoffLimit: 4
```

❶ Specifying a Kubernetes Job.

❷ Name of the job.

❸ Number of times that the pod needs to run successfully before the job is considered completed.

❹ How many pods should run in parallel.

❺ Name of the associated gRPC client container.

❻ Container image that this job is associated with.

Then you can deploy the Job for the gRPC client application using `kubectl apply -f client/grpc-prodinfo-client-job.yaml` and check the status of the pod.

Successful completion of the execution of this Job sends an RPC to add a product in our `ProductInfo` gRPC service. So you can observe the logs for both server and client pods to see whether we get the expected information.

Then we can proceed to exposing your gRPC services outside the Kubernetes cluster using ingress resources.

Kubernetes Ingress for exposing a gRPC service externally

So far what we have done is deploy a gRPC server on Kubernetes and make it accessible to another pod (which is running as a Job) running in the same cluster. What if we want to expose the gRPC service to the external applications outside the Kubernetes cluster? As you learned, the Kubernetes service construct is only meant to expose given Kubernetes pods to the other pods running in the cluster. So, the Kubernetes service is not accessible by the external applications that are outside the Kubernetes cluster. Kubernetes gives another abstraction called an *ingress* to serve this purpose.

We can think of an ingress as a load balancer that sits between the Kubernetes service and the external applications. `Ingress` routes the external traffic to the service; the service then routes the internal traffic between the matching pods. An ingress controller manages the ingress resource in a given Kubernetes cluster. The type and the behavior of the ingress controller may change based on the cluster you use. Also, when you expose a gRPC service to the external application, one of the mandatory requirements is to support gRPC routing at the ingress level. Therefore, we need to select an ingress controller that supports gRPC.

For this example, we'll use the Nginx (*https://oreil.ly/0UC0a*) ingress controller, which is based on the Nginx (*https://www.nginx.com*) load balancer. (Based on the Kubernetes cluster you use, you may select the most appropriate ingress controller that supports gRPC.) Nginx Ingress (*https://oreil.ly/wZo5w*) supports gRPC for routing external traffic into internal services.

So, to expose our `ProductInfo` gRPC server application to the external world (i.e., outside the Kubernetes cluster), we can create an `Ingress` resource as shown in Example 7-7.

Example 7-7. Kubernetes Ingress resource of a Go gRPC server application

```
apiVersion: extensions/v1beta1
kind: Ingress ❶
metadata:
  annotations: ❷
    kubernetes.io/ingress.class: "nginx"
    nginx.ingress.kubernetes.io/ssl-redirect: "false"
    nginx.ingress.kubernetes.io/backend-protocol: "GRPC"
  name: grpc-prodinfo-ingress ❸
spec:
  rules:
  - host: productinfo ❹
    http:
      paths:
      - backend:
          serviceName: productinfo ❺
          servicePort: grpc ❻
```

❶ Specifying an `Ingress` resource.

❷ Annotations related to Nginx Ingress controller and specifying gRPC as the backend protocol.

❸ Name of the `Ingress` resource.

❹ This is the hostname exposed to the external world.

❺ Name of the associated Kubernetes service.

❻ Name of the service port specified in the Kubernetes service.

You will need to install the Nginx Ingress controller prior to deploying the preceding ingress resource. You can find more details on installing and using the Nginx Ingress with gRPC in the Ingress-Nginx (*https://oreil.ly/l-vFp*) repository of Kubernetes. Once you deploy this `Ingress` resource, any external application can invoke the gRPC server via the hostname (`productinfo`) and the default port (80).

With that, you have learned all the fundamentals related to deploying a production-ready gRPC application on Kubernetes. As you have seen, owing to the capabilities that Kubernetes and Docker offer, we don't really have to worry much about most nonfunctional requirements such as scalability, high availability, load balancing, failover, etc., because Kubernetes is providing them as part of the underlying platform. Hence, certain concepts that we learned in Chapter 6, such as load balancing, name resolving at the gRPC code level, etc., are not required if you are running your gRPC applications on Kubernetes.

Once you have a gRPC-based application up and running, you need to ensure the smooth operation of the application in production. To accomplish that goal, you need to consistently observe your gRPC application and take the necessary actions when required. Let's look into the details of the observability aspects of gRPC applications.

Observability

As we discussed in the previous section, gRPC applications are normally deployed and run in containerized environments where there are multiples of such containers running and talking to each other over the network. Then comes the problem of how to keep track of each container and make sure they are actually working. This is where *observability* comes into the picture.

As the Wikipedia definition (*https://oreil.ly/FVPTN*) states, "observability is a measure of how well internal states of a system can be inferred from knowledge of its external outputs." Basically, the purpose of having observability into a system is to answer the question, "Is anything wrong in the system right now?" If the answer is yes, we should also be able to answer a bunch of other questions like "What is wrong?" and "Why is it happening?" If we can answer those questions at any given time and in any part of the system, we can say that our system is observable.

It is also important to note that observability is an attribute of a system that is as important as efficiency, usability, and reliability. So it must be considered from the beginning when we are building gRPC applications.

When talking about observability, there are three main pillars that we normally talk about: metrics, logging, and tracing. These are the main techniques used to gain the observability of the system. Let's discuss each of them separately in the following sections.

Metrics

Metrics are a numeric representation of data measured over intervals of time. When talking about metrics, there are two types of data we can collect. One is system-level metrics like CPU usage, memory usage, etc. The other one is application-level metrics like inbound request rate, request error rate, etc.

System-level metrics are normally captured when the application is running. These days, there are lots of tools to capture those metrics, and they're usually captured by the DevOps team. But application-level metrics differ between applications. So when designing a new application, it is the task of an application developer to decide what kind of application-level metrics need to be captured to get an understanding of the behavior of a system. In this section, we are going to focus on how to enable application-level metrics in our applications.

OpenCensus with gRPC

For gRPC applications, there are standard metrics that are provided by the OpenCensus (*https://oreil.ly/EMfF-*) library. We can easily enable them by adding handlers to both the client and server applications. We can also add our own metrics collector (Example 7-8).

 OpenCensus (*https://opencensus.io*) is a set of open source libraries for collecting application metrics and distributed traces; it supports various languages. It collects metrics from the target application and transfers the data to the backend of your choice in real time. Supported backends currently available include Azure Monitor, Datadog, Instana, Jaeger, SignalFX, Stackdriver, and Zipkin. We can also write our own exporter for other backends.

Example 7-8. Enable OpenCensus monitoring for the gRPC Go server

```
package main

import (
  "errors"
  "log"
  "net"
  "net/http"

  pb "productinfo/server/ecommerce"
  "google.golang.org/grpc"
  "go.opencensus.io/plugin/ocgrpc" ❶
  "go.opencensus.io/stats/view"
  "go.opencensus.io/zpages"
  "go.opencensus.io/examples/exporter"
)

const (
  port = ":50051"
)

// server is used to implement ecommerce/product_info.
type server struct {
  productMap map[string]*pb.Product
```

```
}

func main() {
  go func() { ❼
    mux := http.NewServeMux()
    zpages.Handle(mux, "/debug")
    log.Fatal(http.ListenAndServe("127.0.0.1:8081", mux))
  }()

  view.RegisterExporter(&exporter.PrintExporter{}) ❷

  if err := view.Register(ocgrpc.DefaultServerViews...); err != nil { ❸
    log.Fatal(err)
  }

  grpcServer := grpc.NewServer(grpc.StatsHandler(&ocgrpc.ServerHandler{})) ❹
  pb.RegisterProductInfoServer(grpcServer, &server{}) ❺

  lis, err := net.Listen("tcp", port)
  if err != nil {
    log.Fatalf("Failed to listen: %v", err)
  }

  if err := grpcServer.Serve(lis); err != nil { ❻
    log.Fatalf("failed to serve: %v", err)
  }
}
```

❶ Specify external libraries we need to add to enable monitoring. gRPC OpenCensus provides a predefined set of handlers to support OpenCensus monitoring. Here we are going to use those handlers.

❷ Register stat exporters to export the collected data. Here we add PrintExporter and it logs exported data to the console. This is only for demonstration purposes; normally it's not recommended that you log all production loads.

❸ Register the views to collect the server request count. These are the predefined default service views that collect received bytes per RPC, sent bytes per RPC, latency per RPC, and completed RPC. We can write our own views to collect data.

❹ Create a gRPC server with a stats handler.

❺ Register our ProductInfo service to the gRPC server.

❻ Start listening to incoming messages on the port (50051).

❼ Starts a z-Pages server. An HTTP endpoint starts with the context of /debug in port 8081 for metrics visualization.

Similar to the gRPC server, we can enable OpenCensus monitoring in gRPC clients using client-side handlers. Example 7-9 provides the code snippet for adding a metrics handler to a gRPC client written in Go.

Example 7-9. Enable OpenCensus monitoring for the gRPC Go server

```go
package main

import (
    "context"
    "log"
    "time"

    pb "productinfo/server/ecommerce"
    "google.golang.org/grpc"
    "go.opencensus.io/plugin/ocgrpc" ❶
    "go.opencensus.io/stats/view"
    "go.opencensus.io/examples/exporter"
)

const (
    address = "localhost:50051"
)

func main() {
    view.RegisterExporter(&exporter.PrintExporter{}) ❷

    if err := view.Register(ocgrpc.DefaultClientViews...); err != nil { ❸
        log.Fatal(err)
    }

    conn, err := grpc.Dial(address, ❹
        grpc.WithStatsHandler(&ocgrpc.ClientHandler{}),
            grpc.WithInsecure(),
            )
    if err != nil {
        log.Fatalf("Can't connect: %v", err)
    }
    defer conn.Close() ❻

    c := pb.NewProductInfoClient(conn) ❺

    .... // Skip RPC method invocation.
}
```

❶ Specify external libraries we need to add to enable monitoring.

❷ Register stats and trace exporters to export the collected data. Here we will add PrintExporter, which logs exported data to the console. This is only for demonstration purposes. Normally it is not recommended to log all production loads.

❸ Register the views to collect server request count. These are the predefined default service views that collect received bytes per RPC, sent bytes per RPC, latency per RPC, and completed RPC. We can write our own views to collect data.

❹ Set up a connection to the server with client stats handlers.

❺ Create a client stub using the server connection.

❻ Close the connection when everything is done.

Once we run the server and client, we can access the server and client metrics through the created HTTP endpoint (e.g., RPC metrics on *http://localhost:8081/debug/rpcz* and traces on *http://localhost:8081/debug/tracez*).

As mentioned before, we can use predefined exporters to publish data to the supported backend or we can write our own exporter to send traces and metrics to any backend that is capable of consuming them.

In the next section we'll discuss another popular technology, Prometheus (*https://prometheus.io*), which is commonly used for enabling metrics for gRPC applications.

Prometheus with gRPC

Prometheus is an open source toolkit for system monitoring and alerting. You can use Prometheus for enabling metrics for your gRPC application using the gRPC Prometheus library (*https://oreil.ly/nm84_*). We can easily enable this by adding an interceptor to both the client and server applications and we can also add our own metrics collector, too.

> Prometheus collects metrics from the target application by calling an HTTP endpoint that starts with the context /metrics. It stores all collected data and runs rules over this data to either aggregate and record new time series from existing data or generate alerts. We can visualize those aggregated results using tools like Grafana (*https://grafana.com*).

Example 7-10 illustrates how to add a metrics interceptor and a custom metrics collector to our product management server written in Go.

Example 7-10. Enable Prometheus monitoring for the gRPC Go server

```go
package main

import (
  ...
  "github.com/grpc-ecosystem/go-grpc-prometheus" ❶
  "github.com/prometheus/client_golang/prometheus"
  "github.com/prometheus/client_golang/prometheus/promhttp"
)

var (
  reg = prometheus.NewRegistry() ❷

  grpcMetrics = grpc_prometheus.NewServerMetrics() ❸

  customMetricCounter = prometheus.NewCounterVec(prometheus.CounterOpts{
      Name: "product_mgt_server_handle_count",
      Help: "Total number of RPCs handled on the server.",
  }, []string{"name"}) ❹
)

func init() {
    reg.MustRegister(grpcMetrics, customMetricCounter) ❺
}

func main() {
  lis, err := net.Listen("tcp", port)
  if err != nil {
     log.Fatalf("failed to listen: %v", err)
  }

  httpServer := &http.Server{
      Handler: promhttp.HandlerFor(reg, promhttp.HandlerOpts{}),
        Addr:  fmt.Sprintf("0.0.0.0:%d", 9092)} ❻

  grpcServer := grpc.NewServer(
     grpc.UnaryInterceptor(grpcMetrics.UnaryServerInterceptor()), ❼
  )

  pb.RegisterProductInfoServer(grpcServer, &server{})
  grpcMetrics.InitializeMetrics(grpcServer) ❽

  // Start your http server for prometheus.
  go func() {
     if err := httpServer.ListenAndServe(); err != nil {
        log.Fatal("Unable to start a http server.")
     }
  }()

  if err := grpcServer.Serve(lis); err != nil {
     log.Fatalf("failed to serve: %v", err)
```

```
    }
}
```

❶ Specifies external libraries we need to add to enable monitoring. The gRPC ecosystem provides a predefined set of interceptors to support Prometheus monitoring. Here we are going to use those interceptors.

❷ Creates a metrics registry. This holds all data collectors registered in the system. If we need to add a new collector, we need to register it in this registry.

❸ Creates standard client metrics. These are the predefined metrics defined in the library.

❹ Creates a custom metrics counter with the name `product_mgt_server_han dle_count`.

❺ Registers standard server metrics and custom metrics collector to the registry created in step 2.

❻ Creates an HTTP server for Prometheus. An HTTP endpoint starts with the context `/metrics` on port 9092 for metrics collection.

❼ Creates a gRPC server with a metrics interceptor. Here we use `grpcMetrics.Unar yServerInterceptor`, since we have unary service. There is another interceptor called `grpcMetrics.StreamServerInterceptor()` for streaming services.

❽ Initializes all standard metrics.

Using the custom metrics counter created in step 4, we can add more metrics for monitoring. Let's say we want to collect how many products with the same name are added to our product management system. As shown in Example 7-11, we can add a new metric to `customMetricCounter` in the `addProduct` method.

Example 7-11. Add new metrics to the custom metric counter

```
// AddProduct implements ecommerce.AddProduct
func (s *server) AddProduct(ctx context.Context,
    in *pb.Product) (*wrapper.StringValue, error) {
    customMetricCounter.WithLabelValues(in.Name).Inc()
    ...
}
```

Similar to the gRPC server, we can enable Prometheus monitoring in gRPC clients using client-side interceptors. Example 7-12 provides the code snippet for adding a metrics interceptor to the gRPC client written in Go.

Example 7-12. Enable Prometheus monitoring for the gRPC Go client

```go
package main

import (
  ...
  "github.com/grpc-ecosystem/go-grpc-prometheus" ❶
  "github.com/prometheus/client_golang/prometheus"
  "github.com/prometheus/client_golang/prometheus/promhttp"
)

const (
  address = "localhost:50051"
)

func main() {
  reg := prometheus.NewRegistry() ❷
  grpcMetrics := grpc_prometheus.NewClientMetrics() ❸
  reg.MustRegister(grpcMetrics) ❹

  conn, err := grpc.Dial(address,
        grpc.WithUnaryInterceptor(grpcMetrics.UnaryClientInterceptor()), ❺
          grpc.WithInsecure(),
          )
  if err != nil {
     log.Fatalf("did not connect: %v", err)
  }
  defer conn.Close()

  // Create a HTTP server for prometheus.
  httpServer := &http.Server{
        Handler: promhttp.HandlerFor(reg, promhttp.HandlerOpts{}),
          Addr: fmt.Sprintf("0.0.0.0:%d", 9094)} ❻

  // Start your http server for prometheus.
  go func() {
        if err := httpServer.ListenAndServe(); err != nil {
            log.Fatal("Unable to start a http server.")
        }
  }()

  c := pb.NewProductInfoClient(conn)
  ...
}
```

❶ Specifies external libraries we need to add to enable monitoring.

❷ Creates a metrics registry. Similar to server code, this holds all data collectors registered in the system. If we need to add a new collector, we need to register it to this registry.

❸ Creates standard server metrics. These are the predefined metrics defined in the library.

❹ Registers standard client metrics to the registry created in step 2.

❺ Sets up a connection to the server with the metrics interceptor. Here we use `grpcMetrics.UnaryClientInterceptor`, since we have a unary client. Another interceptor, called `grpcMetrics.StreamClientInterceptor()`, is used for streaming clients.

❻ Creates an HTTP server for Prometheus. An HTTP endpoint starts with the context `/metrics` on port 9094 for metrics collection.

Once we run the server and client, we can access the server and client metrics through the created HTTP endpoint (e.g., server metrics on *http://localhost:9092/metrics* and client metrics on *http://localhost:9094/metrics)*.

As we mentioned before, Prometheus can collect metrics by accessing the preceding URLs. Prometheus stores all metrics data locally and applies a set of rules to aggregate and create new records. And, using Prometheus as a data source, we can visualize metrics in a dashboard using tools like Grafana.

Grafana is an open source metrics dashboard and graph editor for Graphite, Elasticsearch, and Prometheus. It allows you to query, visualize, and understand your metrics data.

One advantage of metrics-based monitoring in the system is that the cost of handling metrics data doesn't increase with the activities of the system. For example, an increase in the application's traffic will not increase handling costs like disk utilization, processing complexity, speed of visualization, operational costs, etc. It has constant overhead. Also, once we collect metrics, we can do numerous mathematical and statistical transformations and create valuable conclusions about the system.

Another pillar of observability is logs, which we'll discuss in the next section.

Logs

Logs are immutable, time-stamped records of discrete events that happened over time. We, as application developers, normally dump data into logs to tell where and what the internal state of the system is at a given point. The benefit of logs is they are the easiest to generate and more granular than metrics. We can attach specific actions or a bunch of context to it like unique IDs, what we are going to do, stack traces, etc.

The downside is that they are very expensive because we need to store and index them in a way that makes it easy to search and use them.

In gRPC applications, we can enable logging using interceptors. As we discussed in Chapter 5, we can attach a new logging interceptor on both the client side and server side and log request and response messages of each remote call.

 The gRPC ecosystem provides a set of predefined logging interceptors for Go applications. This includes grpc_ctxtags, a library that adds a Tag map to context, with data populated from the request body; grpc_zap, integration of the zap (*https://oreil.ly/XMlIg*) logging library into gRPC handlers; and grpc_logrus, integration of the logrus (*https://oreil.ly/oKJX5*) logging library into gRPC handlers. For more information about these interceptors, check out the gRPC Go Middleware repository (*https://oreil.ly/8lNaH*).

Once you add logs in your gRPC application, they'll print in either the console or logfile, depending on how you configure logging. How to configure logging depends on the logging framework you used.

We've now discussed two pillars of observability: metrics and logs. These are sufficient for understanding the performance and behavior of individual systems, but they aren't sufficient to understand the lifetime of a request that traverses multiple systems. Distributed tracing is a technique that brings visibility of the lifetime of a request across several systems.

Tracing

A trace is a representation of a series of related events that constructs the end-to-end request flow through a distributed system. As we discussed in the section "Using gRPC for Microservices Communication" on page 58, in a real-world scenario we have multiple microservices serving different and specific business capabilities. Therefore, a request starting from the client is normally going through a number of services and different systems before the response going back to the client. All these intermediate events are part of the request flow. With tracing, we gain visibility into both the path traversed by a request as well as the structure of a request.

In tracing, a trace is a tree of *spans*, which are the primary building blocks of distributed tracing. The span contains the metadata about the task, the latency (the time spent to complete the task), and other related attributes of the task. A trace has its own ID called TraceID and it is a unique byte sequence. This traceID groups and distinguishes spans from each other. Let's try to enable tracing in our gRPC application.

Like metrics, the OpenCensus library provides support to enable tracing in gRPC applications. We will use OpenCensus to enable tracing in our Product Management application. As we said earlier, we can plug any supported exporters to export tracing data to different backends. We will use Jaeger for the distributed tracing sample.

By default, tracing is enabled in gRPC Go. So it only requires registering an exporter to start collecting traces with gRPC Go integration. Let's initiate a Jaeger exporter in both client and server applications. Example 7-13 illustrates how we can initiate the OpenCensus Jaeger exporter using the library.

Example 7-13. Initialize OpenCensus Jaeger exporter

```
package tracer

import (
  "log"

  "go.opencensus.io/trace" ❶
  "contrib.go.opencensus.io/exporter/jaeger"

)

func initTracing() {

  trace.ApplyConfig(trace.Config{DefaultSampler: trace.AlwaysSample()})
  agentEndpointURI := "localhost:6831"
  collectorEndpointURI := "http://localhost:14268/api/traces" ❷
   exporter, err := jaeger.NewExporter(jaeger.Options{
          CollectorEndpoint: collectorEndpointURI,
          AgentEndpoint: agentEndpointURI,
          ServiceName:    "product_info",

  })
  if err != nil {
     log.Fatal(err)
  }
  trace.RegisterExporter(exporter) ❸

}
```

❶ Import the OpenTracing and Jaeger libraries.

❷ Create the Jaeger exporter with the collector endpoint, service name, and agent endpoint.

❸ Register the exporter with the OpenCensus tracer.

Once we register the exporter with the server, we can instrument the server by tracing. Example 7-14 illustrates how to instrument tracing in service method.

Example 7-14. Instrument gRPC service method

```
// GetProduct implements ecommerce.GetProduct
func (s *server) GetProduct(ctx context.Context, in *wrapper.StringValue) (
        *pb.Product, error) {
  ctx, span := trace.StartSpan(ctx, "ecommerce.GetProduct") ❶
  defer span.End() ❷
  value, exists := s.productMap[in.Value]
  if exists {
     return value, status.New(codes.OK, "").Err()
  }
  return nil, status.Errorf(codes.NotFound, "Product does not exist.", in.Value)
}
```

❶   Start new span with span name and context.

❷   Stop the span when everything is done.

Similar to the gRPC server, we can instrument the client by tracing as shown in Example 7-15.

Example 7-15. Instrument gRPC client

```
package main

import (
  "context"
  "log"
  "time"

  pb "productinfo/client/ecommerce"
  "productinfo/client/tracer"
  "google.golang.org/grpc"
  "go.opencensus.io/plugin/ocgrpc" ❶
  "go.opencensus.io/trace"
  "contrib.go.opencensus.io/exporter/jaeger"

)

const (
  address = "localhost:50051"
)

func main() {
  tracer.initTracing() ❷

  conn, err := grpc.Dial(address, grpc.WithInsecure())
  if err != nil {
     log.Fatalf("did not connect: %v", err)
  }
```

```
    defer conn.Close()
    c := pb.NewProductInfoClient(conn)

    ctx, span := trace.StartSpan(context.Background(),
            "ecommerce.ProductInfoClient") ❸

    name := "Apple iphone 11"
    description := "Apple iphone 11 is the latest smartphone,
            launched in September 2019"
    price := float32(700.0)
    r, err := c.AddProduct(ctx, &pb.Product{Name: name,
        Description: description, Price: price}) ❺
    if err != nil {
        log.Fatalf("Could not add product: %v", err)
    }
    log.Printf("Product ID: %s added successfully", r.Value)

    product, err := c.GetProduct(ctx, &pb.ProductID{Value: r.Value}) ❻
    if err != nil {
        log.Fatalf("Could not get product: %v", err)
    }
    log.Printf("Product: ", product.String())
    span.End() ❹

}
```

❶ Import the OpenTracing and Jaeger libraries.

❷ Call the initTracing function and initialize the Jaeger exporter instance and register with trace.

❸ Start new span with span name and context.

❹ Stop the span when everything is done.

❺ Invoke addProduct remote method by passing new product details.

❻ Invoke getProduct remote method by passing productID.

Once we run the server and client, trace spans are published to the Jaeger agent for which a daemon process acts as a buffer to abstract out batch processing and routing from the clients. Once the Jaeger agent receives trace logs from the client, it forwards them to the collector. The collector processes the logs and stores them. From the Jaeger server, we can visualize tracing.

From that, we are going to conclude the discussion of observability. Logs, metrics, and traces serve their own unique purpose, and it's better to have all three pillars enabled in your system to gain maximum visibility of the internal state.

Once you have a gRPC-based observable application running in production, you can keep watching its state and easily find out whenever there is an issue or system outage. When you diagnose an issue in the system, it is important to find the solution, test it, and deploy it to production as soon as possible. To accomplish that goal, you need to have good debugging and troubleshooting mechanisms. Let's look into the details of these mechanisms for gRPC applications.

Debugging and Troubleshooting

Debugging and troubleshooting is the process to find out the root cause of a problem and solve the issue that occurred in applications. In order to debug and troubleshoot the issue, we first need to reproduce the same issue in lower environments (referred to as dev or test environments). So we need a set of tools to generate similar kinds of request loads as the production environment.

This process is relatively harder in gRPC services than in the HTTP service, because tools need to support both encoding and decoding messages based on the service definition, and be able to support HTTP/2. Common tools like curl or Postman, which are used to test HTTP services, cannot be used to test gRPC services.

But there are a lot of interesting tools available for debugging and testing gRPC services. You can find a list of those tools in the awesome gRPC repository (*https://oreil.ly/Ki2aZ*). It contains a great collection of resources available for gRPC. One of the most common ways of debugging gRPC applications is by using extra logging.

Enabling Extra Logging

We can enable extra logs and traces to diagnose the problem of your gRPC application. In the gRPC Go application, we can enable extra logs by setting the following environment variables:

```
GRPC_GO_LOG_VERBOSITY_LEVEL=99   ❶
GRPC_GO_LOG_SEVERITY_LEVEL=info  ❷
```

❶ *Verbosity* means how many times any single info message should print every five minutes. The verbosity is set to 0 by default.

❷ Sets log severity level to info. All the informational messages will be printed.

In the gRPC Java application, there are no environment variables to control the log level. We can turn on extra logs by providing a *logging.properties* file with log-level changes. Let's say we want to troubleshoot transport-level frames in our application. We can create a new *logging.properties* file in our application and set the lower log level to a specific Java package (netty transport package) as follows:

```
handlers=java.util.logging.ConsoleHandler
io.grpc.netty.level=FINE
java.util.logging.ConsoleHandler.level=FINE
java.util.logging.ConsoleHandler.formatter=java.util.logging.SimpleFormatter
```

Then start up the Java binary with the JVM flag:

```
-Djava.util.logging.config.file=logging.properties
```

Once we set the lower log level in our application, all the logs in which the level is equal or higher than the configured log level will print in the console/logfile. We can gain valuable insight into the state of the system by reading the logs.

With that, we have covered most of what you should know when running a gRPC application in production.

Summary

Making production-ready gRPC applications requires us to focus on multiple aspects related to application development. We start by designing the service contract and generating code for the service or the client, then implementing our service's business logic. Once we implement the service, we need to focus on the following to make the gRPC application production ready. *Testing* of gRPC server and client applications is essential.

The *deployment* of gRPC applications follows the standard application development methodologies. For local and VM deployments, simply use the generated binaries of the server or client program. You can run gRPC applications as a Docker container, and find the sample standard Dockerfiles for deploying Go and Java applications on Docker. Running gRPC on Kubernetes is similar to standard Kubernetes deployment. When you run a gRPC application on Kubernetes, you use underlying features such as load balancing, high availability, ingress controllers,etc. Making gRPC applications observable is critical to using them in production, and gRPC application-level metrics are often used when gRPC applications operate in production.

In one of the most popular implementations for metrics support in gRPC, the gRPC-Prometheus library, we use an interceptor at the server and client side to collect metrics, while logging in gRPC is also enabled using an interceptor. For gRPC applications in production, you may need to troubleshoot or debug by enabling extra logging. In the next chapter, we'll explore some of the gRPC ecosystem components that are useful in building gRPC applications.

CHAPTER 8

The gRPC Ecosystem

In this chapter, we'll explore some of the projects that are not part of the core gRPC implementation but could be quite useful in building and running gRPC applications for a real-world use case. These projects are part of the gRPC Ecosystem parent project, and none of the technologies mentioned here are mandatory to run gRPC applications. If you have a similar requirement that a given project offers, explore and evaluate those technologies.

Let's begin our discussion with the gRPC gateway.

gRPC Gateway

The gRPC gateway plug-in enables the protocol buffer compiler to read the gRPC service definition and generate a reverse proxy server, which translates a RESTful JSON API into gRPC. This is specifically written for Go, to support invoking gRPC service from both gRPC and HTTP client applications. Figure 8-1illustrates how it provides the ability to invoke gRPC service in both gRPC and RESTful ways.

As shown in the figure, we have a `ProductInfo` service contract and using the contract we build a gRPC service called `ProductInfoService`. Earlier we built a gRPC client to talk with this gRPC service. But here, instead of building a gRPC client we will build a reverse proxy service, which exposes RESTful API for each remote method in the gRPC service and accepts HTTP requests from REST clients. Once it receives an HTTP request, it translates the request into a gRPC message and calls the remote method in the backend service. The response message from the backend server again converts back to an HTTP response and replies to the client.

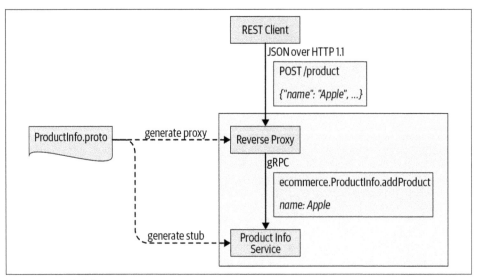

Figure 8-1. gRPC gateway

To generate a reverse proxy service for the service definition, we first need to map the gRPC methods to the HTTP resources by updating the service definition. Let's get the same `ProductInfo` service definition we created, to add mapping entries. Example 8-1 shows the updated protocol buffer definition.

Example 8-1. Updates protocol buffer definition of ProductInfo service

```
syntax = "proto3";

import "google/protobuf/wrappers.proto";
import "google/api/annotations.proto"; ❶

package ecommerce;

service ProductInfo {
   rpc addProduct(Product) returns (google.protobuf.StringValue) {
       option (google.api.http) = { ❷
           post: "/v1/product"
           body: "*"
       };
   }
   rpc getProduct(google.protobuf.StringValue) returns (Product) {
       option (google.api.http) = { ❸
           get:"/v1/product/{value}"
       };
   }
}
```

```
message Product {
    string id = 1;
    string name = 2;
    string description = 3;
    float price = 4;
}
```

❶ Import the *google/api/annotations.proto* proto file to add annotation support to the protocol definition.

❷ Add gRPC/HTTP mapping to the `addProduct` method. Specify the URL path template (`/v1/product`), the HTTP method ("post"), and what the message body looks like. `*` is used in the body mapping to define that every field not bound by the path template should be mapped to the request body.

❸ Add gRPC/HTTP mapping to the `getProduct` method. Here it is a GET method with the URL path template as `/v1/product/{value}` and the `ProductID` passed as the path parameter.

There are additional rules we need to know when we are mapping gRPC methods to HTTP resources. A few important rules are listed next. You can refer to the Google API Documentation (*https://oreil.ly/iYyZC*) for more details about HTTP to gRPC mapping:

- Each mapping needs to specify a URL path template and an HTTP method.
- The path template can contain one or more fields in the gRPC request message. But those fields should be nonrepeated fields with primitive types.
- Any fields in the request message that are not in the path template automatically become HTTP query parameters if there is no HTTP request body.
- Fields that are mapped to URL query parameters should be either a primitive type or a repeated primitive type or a nonrepeated message type.
- For a repeated field type in query parameters, the parameter can be repeated in the URL as `...?param=A&param=B`.
- For a message type in query parameters, each field of the message is mapped to a separate parameter, such as `...?foo.a=A&foo.b=B&foo.c=C`.

Once we write the service definition, we need to compile it using the protocol buffer compiler and generate a source code of reverse proxy service. Let's talk about how to generate code and implement the server in the Go language.

Before we can compile the service definition, we need to get a few dependent packages. Use the following command to download the packages:

```
go get -u github.com/grpc-ecosystem/grpc-gateway/protoc-gen-grpc-gateway
go get -u github.com/grpc-ecosystem/grpc-gateway/protoc-gen-swagger
go get -u github.com/golang/protobuf/protoc-gen-go
```

After downloading the packages, execute the following command to compile the service definition (*product_info.proto*) and to generate the stub:

```
protoc -I/usr/local/include -I. \
-I$GOPATH/src \
-I$GOPATH/src/github.com/grpc-ecosystem/grpc-gateway/third_party/googleapis \
--go_out=plugins=grpc:. \
product_info.proto
```

Once we execute the command, it will generate a stub (*product_info.pb.go*) in the same location. Apart from the generated stub, we also need to create a reverse proxy service to support RESTful client invocation. This reverse proxy service can be generated by the gateway plug-in supported in the Go compiler.

 The gRPC gateway is only supported in Go, which means we cannot compile and generate a reverse proxy service for the gRPC gateway in other languages.

Let's generate a reverse proxy service from service definition by executing the following command:

```
protoc -I/usr/local/include -I. \
-I$GOPATH/src \
-I$GOPATH/src/github.com/grpc-ecosystem/grpc-gateway/third_party/googleapis \
--grpc-gateway_out=logtostderr=true:. \
product_info.proto
```

Once we execute the command, it will generate a reverse proxy service (*product_info.pb.gw.go*) in the same location.

Let's create the listener endpoint for the HTTP server and run the reverse proxy service we just created. Example 8-2 illustrates how to create a new server instance and register the service to listen to the inbound HTTP requests.

Example 8-2. HTTP reverse proxy in Go language

```
package main

import (
  "context"
  "log"
  "net/http"

  "github.com/grpc-ecosystem/grpc-gateway/runtime"
```

```
  "google.golang.org/grpc"

  gw "github.com/grpc-up-and-running/samples/ch08/grpc-gateway/go/gw" ❶
)

var (
  grpcServerEndpoint = "localhost:50051" ❷
)

func main() {
  ctx := context.Background()
  ctx, cancel := context.WithCancel(ctx)
  defer cancel()

  mux := runtime.NewServeMux()
  opts := []grpc.DialOption{grpc.WithInsecure()}
  err := gw.RegisterProductInfoHandlerFromEndpoint(ctx, mux,
      grpcServerEndpoint, opts) ❸
  if err != nil {
    log.Fatalf("Fail to register gRPC gateway service endpoint: %v", err)
  }

  if err := http.ListenAndServe(":8081", mux); err != nil { ❹
    log.Fatalf("Could not setup HTTP endpoint: %v", err)
  }
}
```

❶ Import the package to where the generated reverse-proxy code exists.

❷ Specify the gRPC server endpoint URL. Make sure the backend gRPC server is running properly in the mentioned endpoint. Here we used the same gRPC service created in Chapter 2.

❸ Register the gRPC server endpoint with the proxy handler. At runtime, the request multiplexer matches HTTP requests to patterns and invokes the corresponding handler.

❹ Start listening to the HTTP requests on the port (8081).

Once we build an HTTP reverse-proxy server, we can test it by running both the gRPC server and the HTTP server. In this case, the gRPC server is listening on port 50051 and the HTTP server is listening on port 8081.

Let's make a few HTTP requests from curl and observe the behavior:

1. Add a new product to the ProductInfo service.

```
$ curl -X POST http://localhost:8081/v1/product
        -d '{"name": "Apple", "description": "iphone7", "price": 699}'
```

```
"38e13578-d91e-11e9"
```

2. Get the existing product using `ProductID`:

```
$ curl http://localhost:8081/v1/product/38e13578-d91e-11e9

{"id":"38e13578-d91e-11e9","name":"Apple","description":"iphone7",
"price":699}
```

3. Added to the reverse proxy service, the gRPC gateway also supports generating the swagger definition of the reverse proxy service by executing the following command:

```
protoc -I/usr/local/include -I. \
  -I$GOPATH/src \
  -I$GOPATH/src/github.com/grpc-ecosystem/grpc-gateway/\
  third_party/googleapis \
  --swagger_out=logtostderr=true:. \
  product_info.proto
```

4. Once we execute the command, it generates a swagger definition for the reverse proxy service (*product_info.swagger.json*) in the same location. For our `Produc tInfo` service, generated swagger definition looks like this:

```
{
  "swagger": "2.0",
  "info": {
    "title": "product_info.proto",
    "version": "version not set"
  },
  "schemes": [
    "http",
    "https"
  ],
  "consumes": [
    "application/json"
  ],
  "produces": [
    "application/json"
  ],
  "paths": {
    "/v1/product": {
      "post": {
        "operationId": "addProduct",
        "responses": {
          "200": {
            "description": "A successful response.",
            "schema": {
              "type": "string"
            }
          }
        }
```

```
      },
      "parameters": [
        {
          "name": "body",
          "in": "body",
          "required": true,
          "schema": {
            "$ref": "#/definitions/ecommerceProduct"
          }
        }
      ],
      "tags": [
        "ProductInfo"
      ]
    }
  },
  "/v1/product/{value}": {
    "get": {
      "operationId": "getProduct",
      "responses": {
        "200": {
          "description": "A successful response.",
          "schema": {
            "$ref": "#/definitions/ecommerceProduct"
          }
        }
      },
      "parameters": [
        {
          "name": "value",
          "description": "The string value.",
          "in": "path",
          "required": true,
          "type": "string"
        }
      ],
      "tags": [
        "ProductInfo"
      ]
    }
  }
},
"definitions": {
  "ecommerceProduct": {
    "type": "object",
    "properties": {
      "id": {
        "type": "string"
      },
      "name": {
```

```
          "type": "string"
        },
        "description": {
          "type": "string"
        },
        "price": {
          "type": "number",
          "format": "float"
        }
      }
    }
  }
}
```

So now we have implemented the HTTP reverse proxy service for our gRPC service using the gRPC gateway. This way we can expose our gRPC server to use in HTTP client applications. You can get more information about gateway implementation from the gRPC gateway repository (*https://oreil.ly/rN1WK*).

As we mentioned earlier, the gRPC gateway is only supported in Go. The same concept is also known as HTTP/JSON transcoding. Let's talk more about HTTP/JSON transcoding in the next section.

HTTP/JSON Transcoding for gRPC

Transcoding is the process of translating HTTP JSON calls to RPC calls and passing them to the gRPC service. This is useful when the client applications don't have support for gRPC and need to provide access to talk to the gRPC service via JSON over HTTP. There is a library written in C++ languages to support the HTTP/JSON transcoding called grpc-httpjson-transcoding, and it is currently used in Istio (*https://oreil.ly/vWllM*) and Google cloud endpoint (*https://oreil.ly/KR5_X*).

The Envoy proxy (*https://oreil.ly/33hyY*) also supports transcoding by providing an HTTP/JSON interface to the gRPC service. Similar to the gRPC gateway, we need to provide the service definition with HTTP mapping for the gRPC service. It uses the same mapping rules specified in the Google API documentation (*https://oreil.ly/H6ysW*). So the service definition we modified in Example 8-1 can also be applied to the HTTP/JSON transcoding.

For example, the `Product Info` service's `getProduct` method is defined in the *.proto* file with its request and response types like the following:

```
rpc getProduct(google.protobuf.StringValue) returns (Product) {
    option (google.api.http) = {
        get:"/v1/product/{value}"
    };
}
```

If a client calls this method by sending a GET to the URL http://localhost:8081/v1/product/2, the proxy server creates a *google.protobuf.StringValue* with a value of 2 and then calls the gRPC method `getProduct()` with it. The gRPC backend then returns the requested `Product` with the ID 2, which the proxy server converts to JSON format and returns to the client.

Now that we've covered HTTP/JSON transcoding, in the next section, we'll discuss another important concept, called gRPC server reflection.

The gRPC Server Reflection Protocol

Server reflection is a service defined on a gRPC server that provides information about publicly accessible gRPC services on that server. In simple terms, server reflection provides service definitions of the services registered on a server to the client application. So the client doesn't need precompiled service definitions to communicate with the services.

As we discussed in Chapter 2, for the client application to connect and communicate with the gRPC service, it must have the service definition of that service. We first need to compile the service definition and generate the corresponding client stub. Then we need to create client application calling methods of the stub. With the gRPC server reflection, we don't need to precompile service definitions to communicate with the service.

The service reflection is useful when we build a command-line (CLI) tool for debugging the gRPC server. We don't need to provide service definitions for the tool, but instead we provide the method and the text payload. It sends the binary payload to the server and takes the response back to the user in a human-readable format. In order to use service reflection, we first need to enable it on the server side. Example 8-3 illustrates how to enable server reflection.

Example 8-3. Enable server reflection in the gRPC Go server

```
package main

import (
  ...

  pb "productinfo/server/ecommerce"
  "google.golang.org/grpc"
  "google.golang.org/grpc/reflection" ❶
)

func main() {
  lis, err := net.Listen("tcp", port)
  if err != nil {
```

```
      log.Fatalf("failed to listen: %v", err)
  }
  s := grpc.NewServer()
  pb.RegisterProductInfoServer(s, &server{})
  reflection.Register(s) ❷
  if err := s.Serve(lis); err != nil {
    log.Fatalf("failed to serve: %v", err)
  }
}
```

❶   Import the reflection package to access reflection APIs.

❷   Register reflection service on your gRPC server.

After enabling server reflection in your server application, you can use the gRPC CLI tool to check your server.

 The gRPC CLI tool comes with the gRPC repository. It supports many functionalities, such as the list server services and methods, and sending and receiving RPC calls with metadata. As of this writing, you need to build the tool from the source code. For details on how to build and use the tool, refer to the gRPC CLI tool repository (*https://oreil.ly/jYl0h*).

Once you build the gRPC CLI tool from the source code (*https://github.com/grpc/ grpc*), you can use it to check services. Let's try to understand this using our product management service that we built in Chapter 2. Once you start the gRPC server of the product management service, then you can run the CLI tool to retrieve the service information.

Here are the actions that you can execute from the CLI tool:

List services
    Run the following command to list all public services in endpoint localhost: 50051:

```
    $ ./grpc_cli ls localhost:50051

    Output:
    ecommerce.ProductInfo
    grpc.reflection.v1alpha.ServerReflection
```

List service details
    Run the following command by giving the service's full name (in the format of <package>.<service>) to inspect the service:

```
    $ ./grpc_cli ls localhost:50051 ecommerce.ProductInfo -l
```

```
Output:
package: ecommerce;
service ProductInfo {
rpc addProduct(ecommerce.Product) returns
(google.protobuf.StringValue) {}
rpc getProduct(google.protobuf.StringValue) returns
(ecommerce.Product) {}
}
```

List method details

Run the following command by giving the method's full name (in the format of <package>.<service>.<method>) to method details:

```
$ ./grpc_cli ls localhost:50051 ecommerce.ProductInfo.addProduct -l
```

```
Output:
rpc addProduct(ecommerce.Product) returns
(google.protobuf.StringValue) {}
```

Inspect message types

Run the following commands by giving the full name of the message type (in the format of <package>.<type>) to inspect the message type:

```
$ ./grpc_cli type localhost:50051 ecommerce.Product
```

```
Output:
message Product {
string id = 1[json_name = "id"];
string name = 2[json_name = "name"];
string description = 3[json_name = "description"];
float price = 4[json_name = "price"];
}
```

Call remote methods

Run the following commands to send remote calls to the server and get the response:

1. Call the addProduct method in the ProductInfo service:

   ```
   $ ./grpc_cli call localhost:50051 addProduct "name:
             'Apple', description: 'iphone 11', price: 699"
   ```

   ```
   Output:
   connecting to localhost:50051
   value: "d962db94-d907-11e9-b49b-6c96cfe0687d"

   Rpc succeeded with OK status
   ```

2. Call getProduct method in the ProductInfo service:

   ```
   $ ./grpc_cli call localhost:50051 getProduct "value:
             'd962db94-d907-11e9-b49b-6c96cfe0687d'"
   ```

```
Output:
connecting to localhost:50051
id: "d962db94-d907-11e9-b49b-6c96cfe0687d"
name: "Apple"
description: "iphone 11"
price: 699

Rpc succeeded with OK status
```

Now we can enable server reflection in the gRPC Go server and test it using the CLI tool. We can also enable server reflection in our gRPC Java server. If you are more familiar with Java, you can refer to the Java samples in the source code repository.

Let's discuss another interesting concept called gRPC middleware.

gRPC Middleware

In basic terms, the *middleware* is a software component in a distributed system that is used to connect different components to route requests generated by the client to the backend server. In gRPC Middleware (*https://oreil.ly/EqnCQ*), we are also talking about running code before and after the gRPC server or client application.

In fact, gRPC middleware is based on the *interceptor* concept that we learned in Chapter 5. It's a Go-based collection of interceptors, helpers, and utils that you will require when building gRPC-based applications. It allows you to apply multiple interceptors at the client or server side as a chain of interceptors. Also, as interceptors are commonly used for implementing common patterns such as auth, logging, message, validation, retries, or monitoring, the gRPC Middleware project acts as the go-to point for such reusable functionalities for Go. In Example 8-4, we have shown the common usage of the gRPC Middleware package. Here we have used it for applying multiple interceptors for both unary and streaming messaging.

Example 8-4. interceptor chaining at the server side with Go gRPC Middleware

```
import "github.com/grpc-ecosystem/go-grpc-middleware"

orderMgtServer := grpc.NewServer(
    grpc.Unaryinterceptor(grpc_middleware.ChainUnaryServer( ❶
        grpc_ctxtags.UnaryServerinterceptor(),
        grpc_opentracing.UnaryServerinterceptor(),
        grpc_prometheus.UnaryServerinterceptor,
        grpc_zap.UnaryServerinterceptor(zapLogger),
        grpc_auth.UnaryServerinterceptor(myAuthFunction),
        grpc_recovery.UnaryServerinterceptor(),
    )),
    grpc.Streaminterceptor(grpc_middleware.ChainStreamServer( ❷
```

```
    grpc_ctxtags.StreamServerInterceptor(),
    grpc_opentracing.StreamServerInterceptor(),
    grpc_prometheus.StreamServerInterceptor,
    grpc_zap.StreamServerInterceptor(zapLogger),
    grpc_auth.StreamServerInterceptor(myAuthFunction),
    grpc_recovery.StreamServerInterceptor(),
)),
)
```

❶ Add a unary interceptor chain for the server.

❷ Add a streaming interceptor chain for the server.

The interceptors are invoked in the same order that they have registered with the Go gRPC Middleware. The project also offers some reusable interceptors for common patterns. Here are some of those common patterns and interceptor implementations:

Auth

grpc_auth
: A customizable (via AuthFunc) piece of auth middleware.

Logging

grpc_ctxtags
: A library that adds a Tag map to context, with data populated from the request body.

grpc_zap
: Integration of zap logging library into gRPC handlers.

grpc_logrus
: Integration of logrus logging library into gRPC handlers.

Monitoring

grpc_prometheus
: Prometheus client-side and server-side monitoring middleware.

grpc_opentracing
: OpenTracing client-side and server-side interceptors with support for streaming and handler-returned tags.

Client

grpc_retry
: A generic gRPC response code retry mechanism, client-side middleware.

Server

`grpc_validator`
> Codegen inbound message validation from *.proto* options.

`grpc_recovery`
> Turn panics into gRPC errors.

`ratelimit`
> gRPC rate-limiting by your own limiter.

The usage of Go gRPC Middleware at the client side is exactly the same. Example 8-5 shows a code snippet of the client-side interceptor chaining with Go gRPC Middleware.

Example 8-5. interceptor chaining at the client side with Go gRPC Middleware

```
import "github.com/grpc-ecosystem/go-grpc-middleware"

clientConn, err = grpc.Dial(
    address,
      grpc.WithUnaryinterceptor(grpc_middleware.ChainUnaryClient(
          monitoringClientUnary, retryUnary)), ❶
      grpc.WithStreaminterceptor(grpc_middleware.ChainStreamClient(
          monitoringClientStream, retryStream)), ❷
)
```

❶ Client-side unary interceptor chaining.

❷ Client-side streaming interceptor chaining.

Similar to the server side, the interceptors are executed in the order that they registered with the client.

Next, we will talk about how we can expose the health status of the gRPC server. In a high-availability system, it is essential to have a way to check the health status of the server, so that we can periodically check and take actions to mitigate the damage.

Health Checking Protocol

gRPC defines a health checking protocol (Health Checking API) that allows the gRPC services to expose the server status so that the consumers can probe the server's health information. The health of the server is determined if the server responds with an *unhealthy* status when it is not ready to handle the RPC or does not respond at all for the health probe request. The client can act accordingly if the response denotes an *unhealthy* status or a response is not received within some time window.

The gRPC Health Checking Protocol defines an API based on gRPC. Then a gRPC service is used as the health checking mechanism for both simple client-to-server scenarios and other control systems such as load balancing. Example 8-6 shows the standard service definition of the gRPC health checking interface.

Example 8-6. gRPC service definition of the Health Checking API

```
syntax = "proto3";

package grpc.health.v1;

message HealthCheckRequest { ❶
  string service = 1;
}

message HealthCheckResponse { ❷
  enum ServingStatus {
    UNKNOWN = 0;
    SERVING = 1;
    NOT_SERVING = 2;
  }
  ServingStatus status = 1;
}

service Health {
  rpc Check(HealthCheckRequest) returns (HealthCheckResponse); ❸

  rpc Watch(HealthCheckRequest) returns (stream HealthCheckResponse); ❹
}
```

❶ The health check request message structure.

❷ The health check response with the serving status.

❸ The client can query the server's health status by calling the Check method.

❹ The client can call the Watch method to perform a streaming health check.

The implementation of the health check service is very similar to any conventional gRPC service. Often you will run a health checking service and related gRPC business services together in the same gRPC server instance using multiplexing (which we discussed in Chapter 5). Since it is a gRPC service, doing a health check is the same as doing normal RPC. It also offers a granular service health semantics that includes details such as per-service health status. Also, it is able to reuse all the existing information on the server and have full control over it.

Based on the server interface shown in Example 8-6, a client can call the Check method (with an optional parameter service name) to check the health status of a particular service or the server.

Additionally, the client can also call the Watch method to perform a streaming health check. This uses a server streaming messaging pattern, which means once the client calls this method, the server starts sending messages indicating the current status and sends subsequent new messages whenever the status changes.

These are the key points to know in the gRPC Health Checking Protocol:

- To serve the status of each service registered in the server, we should manually register all the services, along with their status in the server. We also need to set the server's overall status with an empty service name.

- Each health check request from the client should have a deadline set to it, so the client can determine the server status as unhealthy if the RPC is not finished within the deadline period.

- For each health check request, the client can either set a service name or set as empty. If the request has a service name and it is found in the server registry, a response must be sent back with an HTTP OK status and the status field of the HealthCheckResponse message should be set to the status of the particular service (either SERVING or NOT_SERVING). If the service is not found in the server registry, the server should respond with a NOT_FOUND status.

- If the client needs to query the overall status of the server instead of a specific service, the client can send the request with an empty string value so the server responds back with the server's overall health status.

- If the server doesn't have a health check API, then the client should deal with it themselves.

The health check services are consumed by other gRPC consumer or intermediate subsystems such as load balancers or proxies. Rather than implementing a client from scratch, you can use the existing implementation of health checking clients such as grpc_health_probe.

gRPC Health Probe

The grpc_health_probe (*https://oreil.ly/I84Ui*) is a utility provided by the community to check the health status of a server that exposes its status as a service through the gRPC Health Checking Protocol. It's a generic client that can communicate with the gRPC standard health check service. You can use the grpc_health_probe_ binary as a CLI utility as shown in the following:

```
$ grpc_health_probe -addr=localhost:50051 ❶

healthy: SERVING
$ grpc_health_probe -addr=localhost:50052 -connect-timeout 600ms \
 -rpc-timeout 300ms ❷

failed to connect service at "localhost:50052": context deadline exceeded
exit status 2
```

❶ A health checking request for gRPC server running on localhost port 50051.

❷ A health checking request with few more additional parameters related to the connectivity.

As shown in the preceding CL output, grpc_health_probe_ makes an RPC to / grpc.health.v1.Health/Check. If it then responds with a SERVING status, the grpc_health_probe will exit with success; otherwise, it exits with a nonzero exit code.

If you are running your gRPC applications on Kubernetes, then you can run the grpc_health_probe to check to define Kubernetes's liveness and readiness (*https:// oreil.ly/a7bOC*) checks for your gRPC server pods.

For that, you can bundle the gRPC health probe along with your Docker image as shown following in the Dockerfile snippet:

```
RUN GRPC_HEALTH_PROBE_VERSION=v0.3.0 && \
    wget -qO/bin/grpc_health_probe \
    https://github.com/grpc-ecosystem/grpc-health-probe/releases/download/
        ${GRPC_HEALTH_PROBE_VERSION}/grpc_health_probe-linux-amd64 && \
    chmod +x /bin/grpc_health_probe
```

Then in the Kubernetes deployment's pod specification, you can define livenessP robe and/or readinessProbe like this:

```
spec:
  containers:
  - name: server
    image: "kasunindrasiri/grpc-productinfo-server"
    ports:
    - containerPort: 50051
    readinessProbe:
      exec:
        command: ["/bin/grpc_health_probe", "-addr=:50051"] ❶
      initialDelaySeconds: 5
    livenessProbe:
      exec:
        command: ["/bin/grpc_health_probe", "-addr=:50051"] ❷
      initialDelaySeconds: 10
```

❶ Specify `grpc_health_probe` as the readiness probe.

❷ Specify `grpc_health_probe` as the liveness probe.

When you have liveness and readiness probes set using the gRPC health probe, then Kubernetes can make decisions based on the health of your gRPC server.

Other Ecosystem Projects

There are quite a few other ecosystem projects that can be useful when building gRPC-based applications. Customer *protoc* plugging is a similar ecosystem requirement where projects such as *protoc-gen-star (PG*)* (*https://oreil.ly/9eRq8*) started getting some traction. Also, libraries such as *protoc-gen-validate (PGV)* (*https://oreil.ly/KlGy7*) offer a protoc plug-in to generate polyglot message validators. The ecosystem has kept on growing with new projects for various requirements in gRPC application development.

With this, we conclude our discussion of the gRPC ecosystem components. It's important to keep in mind that these ecosystem projects are not part of the gRPC project. You need to evaluate them properly prior to using them in production. Also, these are subject to change: some projects may become obsolete, others may become mainstream, and other, completely new projects, may emerge in the gRPC ecosystem.

Summary

As you can see, though gRPC ecosystem projects are not part of the core gRPC implementation, they can be quite useful in building and running gRPC applications for real-world use cases. These projects are built around gRPC to overcome problems or limitations encountered while building a production system using gRPC. For example, when we are moving our RESTful services to gRPC services, we need to consider our existing client who used to call our service in a RESTful manner. In order to overcome this issue, HTTP/JSON transcoding and gRPC gateway concepts are introduced, so that both existing RESTful clients and new gRPC clients can call the same service. Similarly, service reflection is introduced to overcome the limitation in testing gRPC services using a command-line tool.

Since gRPC is a very popular topic in the cloud-native world and developers are now gradually moving toward gRPC from REST services, we will see more projects like these built around gRPC in the future.

Congratulations! You have just completed reading *gRPC: Up and Running*, and have pretty much covered the entire development life cycle of the gRPC application along with numerous code examples based on Go and Java. We hope this book laid the foundation in the journey of using gRPC as an inter-process communication technology for your applications and microservices. What you learned in this book will help you to rapidly build gRPC applications, understand how they can coexist with other technologies, and run them in production.

So, it's time to explore gRPC further. Try building real-world applications by applying the techniques that you learned in this book. There's a significant amount of features of gRPC that are dependent on the programming language that you use to develop gRPC applications, so you will have to learn certain techniques that are specific to the language that you use. Also, the gRPC ecosystem is exponentially growing and it will be helpful to stay up to date on the latest technologies and frameworks that support gRPC. Go forth and explore!

Index

enabling extra logs/traces, 161
observability, 156

M
marshaling, 8
message
    defining, 21
    encoding using protocol buffers, 63-69
    in HTTP/2, 71
message flow
    bidirectional-streaming RPC, 78
    client-streaming RPC, 78
    client–server, 8
    in gRPC communication patterns, 76-79
    server-streaming RPC, 77
    simple RPC, 76
message framing, length-prefixed, 69-71
metadata, 101-107
    basic authentication and, 125
    creating/retrieving, 102
    name resolver, 106
    sending/receiving: client side, 103
    sending/receiving: server side, 104
metrics
    observability and, 148-156
    OpenCensus with gRPC, 149-152
    Prometheus with gRPC, 152-156
microservices architecture
    defined, 1
    using gRPC for communication, 58-60
middleware, 174-176
mocking, 137
Mockito, 138
modules (Go concept), 26
mTLS (mutual TLS)
    enabling an mTLS secured connection,
        117-122
    enabling in a gRPC client, 120-122
    enabling in a gRPC server, 118-120
multiplexing, 99-101

N
name resolver, 106
Netflix, 16
Nginx, 146
nonvarint numbers, 69

O
OAuth 2.0, 127-130
observability, 148-160
    defined, 148
    logs and, 156
    metrics, 148-156
    tracing and, 157-160
one-way connection
    enabling secured connection in gRPC client,
        116
    enabling secured connection in gRPC
        server, 115
    enabling with TLS, 114-117
OpenCensus
    metrics provided by, 149-152
    tracing support, 157
OpenSSL tool, 114

P
pods, 143
production, running gRPC in, 135-162
    debugging and troubleshooting, 161
    deployment, 139-148
    observability, 148-160
    testing gRPC applications, 135-139
Prometheus, 152-156
protobuf library, 22
protoc, 5, 27, 180
protocol buffers
    about, 4
    defined, 63
    encoding techniques, 67-69
    message encoding with, 63-69
    protoc plug-in, 5
proxy load balancing, 108

R
real-world applications (see application exam-
    ple [online retail system])
remote procedure call (see RPC)
request headers, 73
request message, HTTP/2, 72-74
request-response (synchronous) communica-
    tion style, 2
reserved headers, 74
resource owner, 127
resource server, 127
resource-oriented architecture (ROA), 9

response headers, 75
response message, 74-76
REST (Representation State Transfer), 2, 9-11
    difficulties enforcing architectural style, 10
    inefficient text-based message protocols, 10
    lack of strongly typed interfaces between
        apps, 10
    limitations of, 9-11
RESTful services, 2
reverse proxy service, 163-170
ROA (resource-oriented architecture), 9
RPC (remote procedure call)
    bidirectional-streaming, 53-58, 78
    client-streaming, 49-52, 78
    communication flow, 62-63
    conventional, 8
    server-streaming, 46-49, 77
    simple, 43-46, 76
RSA Key, 114

S

Secure Socket Layer (SSL), 114
security, 113-133
    (see also authentication)
    authenticating a gRPC channel with TLS,
        113-122
    authenticating gRPC calls, 122-132
server, 5
    building with Go, 40
    building with Java, 41
    compression, 111
    creating with Go, 29
    creating with Java, 35
    enabling a one-way secured connection, 115
    enabling mTLS in, 118-120
    error creation/propagation, 96
    interceptor chaining, 174
    Kubernetes deployment resource for, 142
    Kubernetes Ingress for exposing a gRPC
        service externally, 146-147
    Kubernetes Service resource for a gRPC
        server, 144
    metadata: sending/receiving, 104
    running with Go, 40
    running with Java, 41
    testing, 135-137
server reflection protocol, 171-174
server skeleton, 3, 6
server-side interceptors, 82-86

stream interceptor, 84-86
    unary interceptor, 83
server-streaming RPC, 46-49, 77
service
    defining, 22-24
    developing, 25-39
    implementing with Go, 26-30
    implementing with Java, 30-36
Service (Kubernetes abstraction), 144
service definition, 4
    bidirectional-streaming RPC, 54-56
    defining messages, 21
    defining services, 22-24
    for online retail system application, 20-24
service interface, 3
service skeleton, 6
service-oriented architecture (SOA), 9
signed integers, 68
simple RPC, 43-46, 76
SOAP (Simple Object Access Protocol), 9
SSL (Secure Socket Layer), 114
status codes, 95
stream
    defined, 46
    in HTTP/2, 71
stream interceptor
    client-side, 88
    server-side, 84-86
streaming
    bidirectional-streaming RPC, 53-58, 78
    client-streaming RPC, 49-52, 78
    server-streaming RPC, 46-49, 77
string type, 69
symmetric cryptography, 113
synchronous request-response communication
    style, 2
system-level metrics, 149

T

testing, 135-139
    continuous integration, 139
    load testing, 138
    testing a client, 137
    testing a server, 135-137
Thrift (Apache Thrift), 14
timeouts, 90
TLS (Transport Level Security)
    authenticating a gRPC channel with,
        113-122

About the Authors

Kasun Indrasiri is an author and architect with extensive experience in microservices, cloud native and enterprise integration architecture. He is the director of integration architecture at WSO2 and the product manager of the WSO2 Enterprise Integrator. He has authored *Microservices for Enterprise* (Apress, 2018) and has been a speaker at several conferences, including the O'Reilly Software Architecture Conference 2019 in San Jose and GOTO Con 2019 in Chicago, as well as WSO2 Conferences. Kasun lives in San Jose, California, and is the founder of the "Silicon Valley Microservices, APIs and Integration" Meetup, one of the largest microservices meetups in the San Francisco Bay area.

Danesh Kuruppu is an associate technical lead at WSO2 with over five years of experience in enterprise integration and microservices technologies. Danesh is the main designer and developer for adding gRPC support for the open source, cloud native programming language Ballerina. He is part of the gRPC community and a key contributor to the WSO2 Microservices Framework for Java and the WSO2 Governance Registry.

Colophon

The animal on the cover of *gRPC: Up and Running* is the greater American scaup (*Aythya marila*). This duck species breeds in spring and summer in the circumpolar tundra environments of Alaska, Canada, and Europe, then migrates south to winter off the coasts of North America, Europe, and Asia.

Males have yellow eyes, a bright blue bill, an iridescent black head with a distinctly dark green cast, white sides, and finely patterned grey and white feathers on their backs. Females are subtly colored to protect them while nesting, with a pale blue beak and small white face patch, and a brown head and body. These ducks average about 20 inches long with a 30-inch wingspan, and on average weigh two pounds.

Greater American scaups form pairs in spring, and the female lays on average eight eggs in a ground nest lined with down pulled from her own body. The ducklings leave the nest immediately after hatching, and are able to feed themselves from birth. As they take more than forty days to fledge, and though the young birds are protected by their mother, at this time they are vulnerable to birds of prey and terrestrial predators such as foxes.

Scaups are part of a group known as *diving ducks*; though they do feed on land or at the water's surface, they also dive underwater to feed. Like other diving ducks, scaups have legs set further back on their compact bodies to help propel themselves underwater. Their physiology is also adapted so that they use less oxygen during their dives. The greater American scaup can dive to a depth of up to 20 feet, and can hold their breath for about a minute, enabling them to forage at greater depths than some other diving ducks.

Though populations have been declining for the last forty years, these ducks are currently noted as being of "Least Concern" by the IUCN Red List. Many of the animals on O'Reilly covers are endangered; all of them are important to the world.

The color illustration on the cover is by Karen Montgomery, based on a black and white engraving from *British Birds*. The cover fonts are Gilroy Semibold and Guardian Sans. The text font is Adobe Minion Pro; the heading font is Adobe Myriad Condensed; and the code font is Dalton Maag's Ubuntu Mono.

O'REILLY®

There's much more where this came from.

Experience books, videos, live online training courses, and more from O'Reilly and our 200+ partners—all in one place.

Learn more at oreilly.com/online-learning

Milton Keynes UK
Ingram Content Group UK Ltd.
UKHW031104190724
445808UK00008B/149